PREPARATION OF THIS BOOK HAS BEEN MADE POSSIBLE BY GRANTS FROM THE
PHILADELPHIA ELECTRIC COMPANY AND THE PHILADELPHIA SAVING FUND SOCIETY

TREASURES of the

PHILADELPHIA

MUSEUM OF ART

and the John G. Johnson Collection

Philadelphia 1973

Cover: Drawing Room from Lansdowne House, London, 1765–1773. (*See page 60*)

Foreword

With a firm spirit of commitment characteristic of Philadelphia at one of the proudest moments in its history, a group of prominent gentlemen came together in 1875 to organize a new art museum. The impetus had been a decision of the Pennsylvania Legislature whereby the fireproof building being constructed in Fairmount Park as the focal point of the coming Centennial Exhibition should become a permanent memorial of that celebration as an art museum. The Pennsylvania Museum and School of Industrial Art received its charter on February 26, 1876; on May 10, 1877, one year to the day after President Ulysses S. Grant, standing on the steps of Memorial Hall, inaugurated the exposition, Memorial Hall was opened once again—as Philadelphia's new museum.

The Museum was launched with high ideals as a "perpetual" source of "improvement and enjoyment" for the people of the Commonwealth; indeed, according to the charter, the new Museum and School would "develop the Art Industries of the State." As a model for the new institution, the charter cited the best-known public collection of decorative arts at that date, the South Kensington Museum in London (today the Victoria and Albert Museum), which had been created shortly after the close of the famous Crystal Palace Exhibition of 1851. With that example in mind as the Centennial drew to a close, funds were raised locally to purchase for the new Museum a considerable number of the exhibits that had earlier inspired throngs of visitors.

The danger that after the initial enthusiasm the Museum might become little more than a repository of Centennial acquisitions was quickly overcome. Still stirred by the excitement of the Centennial, certain trustees visited a succession of international expositions seeking works that would prove "instructive." On such occasions, for example, John T. Morris bought fine examples of contemporary decorative arts while, with great flair, John H. Converse and Samuel M. Vauclain purchased a Japanese Temple Gate from the Louisiana Purchase Exposition.

The Museum's most distinguished early donor was Mrs. Bloomfield Moore, who in 1882 and 1899 gave in memory of her husband a varied group of fine objects, from paintings and porcelains to books and fans. Within a year of her initial gift, Joseph E. Temple established the Museum's first acquisition fund, thereby constituting a basis for the methodical growth of the collections. Crowning the first phase of the Museum's collecting activity was Mrs. William D. Frishmuth's donation, in 1902 and the following years, of her "Colonial relics," a collection epitomizing the taste of post-Centennial collectors in which distinction was rarely made between curiosity and quality. By this time the cavernous spaces of Memorial Hall were crowded with a startling combination of exhibits ranging from deluxe souvenirs of international travel to spectacular objects of true quality.

An action taken by one person, Mrs. William P. Wilstach, totally revised the philosophy of the Museum: by bequeathing to the Commissioners of Fairmount Park not only her collection of paintings but also a significant sum for its continued growth she assured that pictures would become for the first time an important element in the Museum's collections. When her moneys became available in 1893, a committee, chaired first by the city's most prominent collector, the corporate lawyer John G. Johnson, and later by Joseph E. Widener, used those funds to purchase works of a nature not to be found in Philadelphia's drawing rooms.

The emergence at the turn of the century of a new generation of collectors, now concentrating upon paintings, brought about an increasing awareness that the walls of Memorial Hall were hardly adequate to display all the treasures the Museum might expect to inherit. Therefore, when in the years preceding World War I the great boulevard that connects the city with its vast park was conceived, a monumental classical museum was projected as its terminus. Although discussed as early as 1907, the building was begun only in 1919, on the basis of plans by Horace Trumbauer, C. L. Borie, and C. C. Zantzinger. Fortunately, with as able a President as the distinguished collector John D. McIlhenny, and his successor Eli Kirk Price; with J. Stogdell Stokes nurturing the progress of the structure; and in 1925 with the appointment of the brilliant Fiske Kimball as Director, the opening of the new building was realized on the schedule imposed by the wills of George W. Elkins and his son William and of John H. McFadden. The curiosity of the many Philadelphians who had been watching the dramatic construction of this great building, probably the last major edifice to be erected in America according to classical precepts, assured the Museum's being inundated with large numbers of visitors in the weeks following the official opening on March 26, 1928.

Those first visitors discovered an elegance in the presentation of fine objects which was far removed from what they had grown accustomed to in Memorial Hall; thus the new building on Fairmount quickly became "The Art Museum," although the Museum's study collections continued to be shown in the Centennial structure until 1954.

The first galleries completed presented the philosophy of installation that would eventually characterize the whole Museum. Rather than following the scheme evolved at the 1876 exposition—grouping objects by mediums—in the second-floor galleries pictures, sculpture, and the decorative arts were juxtaposed, all shown sequentially to suggest the evolution of the arts in the East and the West. As often as possible period rooms were incorporated into the plan, giving the installations their distinctive character.

The Great Crash occurred within months of the launching of the new Museum. Just two days before the Crash sufficient funds had been secured from a banking syndicate to reserve the collection of French and Italian Renaissance objects assembled by the French connoisseur Edmond Foulc. Settling that commitment was a binding problem through lean years, but so large a group of brilliant treasures could hardly have been acquired otherwise. In 1933 the realities of the Depression forced the trustees of the John G. Johnson Collection to decide that the paintings must be moved from the house on South Broad Street to the Museum. Fortunately, construction of the interior continued during the 1930s because of federal grants received under the Works Progress Administration.

In the years following the Depression the Museum adopted a policy of accumulating the income of its various funds to concentrate its efforts on certain major acquisitions. Thus, in 1937 Cézanne's *Bathers* was purchased with considerable furor; late in World War II the second collection of medieval material created by the remarkable American sculptor George Grey Barnard was acquired; in 1950, to celebrate the Museum's Diamond Jubilee, important works by Rubens, Le Nain, Corot, and Delacroix were added; and in 1956 the bulk of the Museum's sculpture from the subcontinent of India was purchased.

Understandably, given the outstanding holdings of the Pennsylvania Academy of the Fine Arts the acquisition of American paintings had hardly been pursued. However, attitudes changed abruptly in 1929 when Mrs. Thomas Eakins and Miss Mary A. Williams in a spectacular gesture gave the Museum the works still remaining in the studio of Philadelphia's most distinguished artist. Shortly thereafter Judge Alexander Simpson, Jr., presented his fine group of American paintings, and since then there have been similar gifts from other generous donors—from the heirs of Alfred Stieglitz in 1949 to recent gifts from Colonel and Mrs. Edgar W. Garbisch. Lately, reflecting yet again a trend evident among local collectors, the Museum has acquired works suggesting the vitality of contemporary American art; significant in this new phase have been the funds raised by the Friends of the Museum.

No other major American museum has depended so much upon the incredible generosity of private donors for the growth of its collections. Such leaders in the life of the Museum as the John D. McIlhennys, the R. Sturgis Ingersolls, and the Carroll Tysons have given superb objects enriching many areas. Other collectors have strengthened immeasurably the holdings in specific fields, for example, Mrs. Charles F. Williams's gift of her husband's impressive collection of carpets, Major General and Mrs. William Crozier's gift of Chinese ceramics and rock-crystal carvings, and Eleanore Elkins Rice's bequest of eighteenth-century French decorative arts. In the years following World War I recognition of the discreet opulence of Philadelphia's spectacular eighteenth-century furnishings led many of the city's most distinguished families to bequeath their inherited treasures to the Museum. And, more recently, essentially through the astonishing generosity of just a few collectors—first Louise and Walter Arensberg and Albert E. Gallatin, and then Louis E. Stern and the Samuel S. Whites—the Museum has become admired internationally for its collections of early twentieth-century art.

Over the years many of the donors mentioned have as well provided funds to ensure the continued growth of the Museum, and the expenditure of these funds according to a studied and energetic policy has been one of its greatest challenges. Recently two major funds have come to the Museum, that bequeathed by Mr. and Mrs. Staunton B. Peck for the print collection and, the most considerable fund received to date, that of Fiske and Marie Kimball.

The collections of the Philadelphia Museum of Art do not present a comprehensive history of world art. This is partly the result of the 1941 agreement with the University of Pennsylvania whereby the Philadelphia Museum of Art would collect and exhibit only Western post-Christian art and Oriental art after A.D. 500 (ancient art and the art of other cultures being reserved for the University Museum), partly a reality due to the erratic pattern of growth characteristic of a museum owing so much to the generosity of private collectors. Nevertheless, the illustrations in this volume can leave no doubt that the Museum has been consistent in its dedication to the gathering and exhibition of the finest examples of man's creative genius.

Evan H. Turner, *Director*

Main Reception Hall from the Palace of Duke Chao (Chao Kung Fu), Peking

MING DYNASTY, FIRST HALF OF THE SEVENTEENTH CENTURY

GIVEN BY EDWARD B. ROBINETTE. 29-163-1

According to tradition, the Chief Eunuch of the T'ien Ch'i Emperor built a palace in the north-eastern part of the old Chinese capital of Peking, on land granted to him by the Emperor. This chamber was part of the reception hall, one of many buildings in the palace compound, but the first to be encountered by the visitor. Here, seated on a throne between two red-lacquered columns, the Chief Eunuch would most likely have received guests and petitioners. The hall, unique in the United States, is a noble example of Chinese architecture. Its wooden roof structure, left exposed as is typical of many buildings of the Far East, is emphasized by the painted decoration of floral, animal, and conventional motifs such as the flowers of the four seasons; dragons, the symbol of the Emperor; and ch'i-lins, fabulous creatures signifying longevity and happiness.

Bottle, CHINESE, YÜAN DYNASTY, EARLY FOURTEENTH CENTURY

PORCELAIN, DECORATED IN UNDERGLAZE BLUE, HEIGHT 12⅝″
PURCHASED: JOHN T. MORRIS FUND. 52-30-1

The Chinese name for this form of wine bottle, *yu-hu ch'un p'ing*, translated literally as "spring in a jade jar," is the same as that of a wine popular in China over a thousand years ago, which it might once have contained. Chinese potters, who were the first to produce porcelain, also perfected the art of decorating it with designs painted in cobalt blue and covered with a transparent glaze. Whether the craftsman who formed the elegant shape in two sections on a potter's wheel and then luted the top and bottom together at the widest point of its contour was the same as the artist who applied the pale-blue decoration will never be known. Certainly the hand that painted the flowering plants (peonies, chrysanthemums, pomegranates, and camellias) surrounding the rocks and added the delicately drawn bamboo—almost as a signature—was that of a master.

Bust of a Bodhisattva, CHINESE, ABOUT 530

MARBLE, HEIGHT 11½″
GIVEN BY MR. AND MRS. JOHN S. JENKS. 27·20·16

The town of Ting Chou, southwest of Peking in Hopei Province, was a center for religious carving, probably because it was the source of beautiful marble. Although this Buddhist sculpture from Ting Chou is fragmentary, it is one of the finest known examples of Chinese religious sculpture. We see it now as it was when the sculptor created a reverent image from white micaceous marble, that is, before it was painted and gilded. And in this pristine state, as an example of the carver's art, it can easily stand comparison with the greatest products of medieval Christian workmanship.

Grave Pillow, CHINESE, SUNG DYNASTY (960–1279)

GREEN CHÜN WARE (PORCELANEOUS STONEWARE), HEIGHT 4¾"
GIVEN BY MAJOR GENERAL AND MRS. WILLIAM CROZIER. 44-20-97

During the Northern Sung Dynasty, the town of Chün Chou in northern Honan Province was the production center for blue- and green-glazed stoneware. This grave pillow was molded in the symbolic form of a fungus (*ju-i*, which in Chinese also means "as you wish") probably with the hope that the deceased in whose tomb it would be used would be content in the afterlife. Certainly the glaze covering the top and sides is most satisfying to the eye. Thick and green, it encloses millions of tiny bubbles which refract light through its glassy body.

Red Camellia, CHINESE, EARLY MING DYNASTY, FIFTEENTH CENTURY

ALBUM PAINTING, WATERCOLOR ON SILK, 10⅛ × 10⅛″
PURCHASED. 29-40-1

Although this painting bears the signature of Wu Ping (active 1190–1194), a celebrated flower painter of the Southern Sung Dynasty, more likely it was painted by an anonymous fifteenth-century artist who was either trying to emulate the style of the earlier master or copying, for preservation, an original painting by him. The single full-blown red camellia appears almost as if freshly cut from the shrub and laid across the album page, its beauty to be recorded before it fades. With opaque color washes and very little shading, the painter has captured the essence of the camellia, what the Chinese call *ch'a hua*, or tea flower, the tea plant being closely related to the camellia.

11

Hsü Wei (CHINESE, 1521–1593)
Sixteen Flowers

HANGING SCROLL, INK ON PAPER,
10′11″ × 3′3″
PURCHASED: FISKE AND MARIE KIMBALL
FUND. 68-29-1

Hsü Wei was what one would consider a "colorful character." Born in a province along the central coast of China, he was not only a brilliant scholar, an official of merit, and a respected artist, poet, and calligrapher but also a winebibber, a rugged individual, and a criminal, having murdered his wife in a fit of jealousy. However, these facts of the artist's life can only support the evidence of individuality and talent that are so obvious in this great painting. Executed with a masterful control of the brush—"written" truly with spirit and speed—it is an expression of a T'ang Dynasty poem about a fabulous gardener who was able to force flowers of all seasons to bloom at one time, about which Hsü Wei himself has written a poem at the upper right of the scroll. In this painting the artist also brings into bloom at once sixteen flowers from all the seasons.

Yi Om (KOREAN, BORN 1499)
Puppy Playing with a Pheasant Feather

HANGING SCROLL, WATERCOLOR AND INK ON SILK, 12 1/8 × 17 1/8"
PURCHASED. 59-105-1

About Yi Om, whose pen name was Tusongyong, and whose seal appears on this painting, there
is little recorded, but one can see from a glance at this enchanting painting that he not only loved
animals but also closely observed their moods and motions. One can hardly fail to smile in instant
recognition of a frisky, happy puppy, slightly unsure of foot, who has found a feather to play with.
Certainly this beguiling puppy is not fleet enough to have acquired his plaything directly from
its original owner.

13

Dog Cage, CHINESE, CH'ING DYNASTY, CH'IEN LUNG PERIOD (1736–1795)

BRASS AND CLOISONNÉ, HEIGHT 45½"
GIVEN BY THE FRIENDS OF THE MUSEUM. 64-205-1

A pampered Pekingese pug dog no doubt lived in the imperial palace and was trundled around in this palace-on-wheels by ladies of the court. His fine porcelain food and water dishes are gone from it, as are the silk tapestry curtains that hung from hooks in the lion's-head bosses, but the resplendent cage remains to show how these small pets were beloved and cared for by members of the Chinese imperial family. Under the central finial of the roof is inscribed a four-character mark of the Ch'ien Lung Emperor, and five-clawed imperial dragons cavort in the cloisonné decoration and stand guard around the roof.

Moon Crystal, CHINESE, CH'ING DYNASTY, CH'IEN LUNG PERIOD (1736–1795)

ROCK CRYSTAL, HEIGHT 10 ⅞″
GIVEN BY MAJOR GENERAL AND MRS. WILLIAM CROZIER. 44-20-8

This superb rock-crystal moon is said to have come from the collection of the Ch'ien Lung Emperor, an avid patron and collector of the arts. Skillful carving of rock crystal such as this was a development of the Ch'ing Dynasty (1644–1911) that was probably encouraged by the Emperor himself. From a remarkably flawless piece of quartz, an anonymous artist has produced a beautiful representation of an old Taoist legend which tells of a white hare who lives in the moon and pounds the drugs that make up the elixir of life. Clouds scud across the face of the moon, which is supported on a base in the form of a hare busily at work. A poem about the moon by Hsieh Chuang (421–466) was inscribed on the surface by Chao P'ing-chung.

Shinto Deity, JAPANESE, FUJIWARA PERIOD, ELEVENTH OR TWELFTH CENTURY

CAMPHOR WOOD, ORIGINALLY PAINTED, HEIGHT 39"
PURCHASED: J. STOGDELL STOKES FUND. 65-25-1

Shinto, or "The Way of the Gods," is the term by which the native Japanese religion came to be known after the introduction of Buddhism in the sixth century A.D. While Shinto was a pantheistic and loosely structured religion, lacking any canons or iconography, the influence of Buddhism, especially during the eighth and ninth centuries, resulted in an iconographic fusion of the two religions, with Shinto deities becoming identified with Buddhist ones. It is from this period that the first Shinto images date. This statue, carved approximately two hundred years later, does not differ substantially from earlier ones in style and conception; but it is distinguished from contemporary Buddhist sculpture by its truly striking simplicity and an aura of timeless monumentality. It is not possible to identify this deity with certainty, for many male deities were conventionally depicted with an eight-pointed crown and simple robe. At one time the entire figure must have been vividly painted, but only traces of black paint on the hair and eyebrows now remain.

Leaf from a Poetry Anthology, JAPANESE, HEIAN PERIOD, 1108–1112

ALBUM LEAF, MOUNTED AS A HANGING SCROLL, INK AND PAINT OVER
WOOD-BLOCK PRINT ON COATED PAPER, 8 × 6¼"
PURCHASED: JOHN T. MORRIS FUND. 65·77·1

A design of chrysanthemums and plum blossoms printed in a white ink made of shimmering ground mica decorates the paper on which this elegant cursive script is written. The page is also embellished with delicately painted pine branches, bellflowers, wisteria, cherry and maple leaves, and birds. It originally formed part of a sumptuous edition of the "Anthology of Poems by Thirty-Six Poets" (*Sanjū-rokunin shū*) made for Emperor Shirakawa (reigned 1074–1129) on the occasion of his sixtieth birthday in 1112, on which some twenty leading calligraphers labored. A poem about love composed by Lady Ise (died about 940) as well as two partial poems by her appear on this page, which exemplifies the elegance of calligraphic line and the fine workmanship typical of the entire anthology. While the name of the calligrapher of this section is not known, there is no doubt that he ranked among the best of his time.

Scene from the Biography of Kōnin Shōnin, JAPANESE, KAMAKURA PERIOD, EARLY FOURTEENTH CENTURY

SECTION OF A HANDSCROLL, MOUNTED AS A HANGING SCROLL, WATERCOLOR ON PAPER, 13½ × 21⅛"
GIVEN BY MRS. MONCURE BIDDLE, IN MEMORY OF HER FATHER, ERNEST F. FENOLLOSA. 62-18-1

The Japanese handscroll, one of the most refined forms of narrative art, consists of a series of scenes viewed in sequence, one at a time, as the scroll is unrolled from right to left. The subjects of the scrolls—some of them over thirty feet in length—are either secular themes taken from literature and history, or religious scenes such as the biographies of famous priests or the history of a temple. The handscroll to which this scene and another in the Museum collections once belonged, and which depicted incidents from the life of the priest Kōnin Shōnin, comes from a provincial temple known as Jinoji. The narrative originally formed two scrolls having a total of thirteen episodes. This scene from the last part of the second scroll shows Kōnin Shōnin meditating on a cliff, isolated from worldly cares, and exemplifies the Buddhist monastic tradition of solitude and harmony with nature.

Sōsen (JAPANESE, ACTIVE KANEI ERA, 1624–1643)

Flowers of the Four Seasons

DETAIL OF A HANDSCROLL, COLORS ON PAPER, HEIGHT 11½"
GIVEN BY MRS. JOHN C. ATWOOD, JR. 65-21-1

Although almost nothing is known about the life of the artist Sōsen, except that he belonged to the Rimpa, or decorative school, and was active during the Kanei Era, this lovely handscroll attests to his great talent. Throughout the scroll he skillfully uses contrasting colors and lines to give direction to what could have been an essentially static subject. The tenuous plum blossoms and narcissus of late winter lead to May-blooming wisteria, with dandelions in flower near its stem. In this detail, June iris and yellow spatterdock (a variety of water plant) crowd in and suggest the progress of natural growth, quickening with summer. These are followed by peonies, vines, autumn grasses, and morning glories.

Ike no Taiga (JAPANESE, 1723–1776)

Flowering Plum Trees in Mist

PAIR OF SIX-FOLD SCREENS, INK AND SLIGHT GOLD WASH ON PAPER, EACH 5′ × 11′9¼″
PURCHASED: THE GEORGE W. ELKINS COLLECTION. E 69-1-1, 2

The hardy flowering plum is the first tree to bloom in late winter, its lightly scented blossoms appearing often before the snows have melted, and is thus a symbol in the Far East of the reawakening of nature and the coming of spring. In this magnificent pair of screens painted with flowering plum trees, Ike no Taiga has successfully depicted the different textures of their aged, gnarled wood, their delicate young blossoms, and the firm new shoots growing among jagged rocks. The composition shows a subtle balance between the darker, more massive rocks and branches of the right screen and the light-hued washes and large open space seen on the left. The stippled effect of the blossoms conveys their fragility and lends a quality of surprising lightness and movement to these large screens. The way in which Ike no Taiga has captured the essence of the flowering plum is indisputable proof of his rare sensitivity to nature and his artistic genius.

Temple of the Attainment of Happiness (Shōfukuji), from Nara Prefecture, Japan
MUROMACHI PERIOD, 1398, WITH LATER RESTORATIONS

PURCHASED. 29-58-1

The Buddhist Shōfukuji Temple, founded in 1398, stands in Katagiri village in Nara Prefecture, about three miles from the famous Hōryūji Temple, which administers it. Extensively repaired in the seventeenth century, this building from the temple complex was dismantled in 1928 and later reassembled in the Museum according to the original plan (but with a new tile roof, made in the traditional style). It is supported by twelve cypress posts resting on stone bases, with white plaster walls on three sides and three wooden latticed doors at the front. Within the temple, images and objects of Buddhist ritual are arranged for worship. At the center is the main altar, open on three sides, on which is a seventeenth-century lacquered and gilded statue of Amida Buddha, Lord of the Western Paradise. In front are ceremonial objects of the esoteric Shingon sect, such as temple banners, copper vases holding brass lotus flowers, an incense burner, and an altar table with bells, candle holders, and other utensils.

Nō Robe, JAPANESE, EDO PERIOD, EIGHTEENTH CENTURY

PLAIN SILK CLOTH, EMBROIDERED AND GOLD STAMPED
GIVEN BY J. C. LEFF. 53-21-2

The Japanese Nō theater is an aristocratic, highly stylized dramatic form. A single pine tree is painted on the wooden back wall of the Nō stage, and props are no more than symbolic representations. The masked actors use measured, formalized gestures while delivering their poetic lines. In contrast to this severity are the sumptuous costumes worn by even the humblest characters. Selection of costumes is left up to the individual actor, but various distinguishing features of weave, color, and design determine the general category of role for which a specific robe may be used. This robe is of the *atsuita* ("thick board") type, named for its stiff silk, and is usually worn by the protagonist in so-called "warrior" plays. On a brilliant red ground is an asymmetrical design of garden boxes, containing arrangements of autumn flowers—chrysanthemums, bellflowers, and bush clover. The boxes and flowers are embroidered, while the overall pattern of grasses and dewdrops is stamped in gold.

Ceremonial Teahouse from Tokyo, ABOUT 1917

PURCHASED. 28-114-1

This teahouse, built in the traditional style called *sukiya-tsukuri* ("artless building"), expresses the simplicity, restraint, harmony, and detachment from the world embodied in the spirit of the Japanese tea ceremony. Its seeming artlessness, in fact, conceals an acute attention to detail and refined aesthetic pleasure. The architecture reveals a special delight in natural materials—thatch, wood, bamboo, and earth-colored plaster—and closeness to nature is emphasized by its situation in a garden. Inside, everything has been planned to stimulate the mind and delight the eye: rough vertical posts remind man of his own imperfection and his oneness with nature; the calligraphy on the scroll admonishes him to "Look to where you stand"; and the utensils (iron water kettle, bamboo ladle, lacquer tea caddy, and pottery bowl) enhance his sensitivity to natural textures and artistic creativity. The tea ceremony is designed to make the participants conscious of the pleasures to be derived from such a simple pastime as drinking tea, offering temporary refuge from the complexities of daily life. This mood is perhaps what inspired an earlier tea-cult devotee to inscribe the tablet under the eaves with the words *sun ka raku* ("evanescent joys").

Avalokiteshvara, CAMBODIAN, KHMER EMPIRE,
PRE-ANGKOR PERIOD, LATE SEVENTH CENTURY

SANDSTONE, HEIGHT 69¾"
PURCHASED: THE W. P. WILSTACH
COLLECTION. W 65-1-1

An unknown master sculptor who must have been a devout follower of the teachings of Mahayana Buddhism created this figure for worship. In the form of a serene and smiling youth, Avalokiteshvara, the Lord of Mercy, stands looking down from under half-closed lids upon the spectator with what seems an expression of ineffable compassion. This has been called one of the finest works in the entire range of Khmer art. And certainly it is one of the most beautiful. The subtle understatement of the soft modeling of the body and the lightly incised details of his garment, the *paridhana*, focus attention on the face of the deity, who has been evoked for the worshiper in the form of a benign young man.

Nandi, INDIAN, FROM MYSORE, HOYSALA DYNASTY, THIRTEENTH CENTURY

INDURATED POTSTONE, LENGTH 31¾"
PURCHASED: JOSEPH E. TEMPLE FUND. 66-123-1

Nandi ("Joy") is the name of the Indian humped or zebu bull, which when represented in art conveys the presence of the god Shiva. The image of Nandi is the foremost subject of Indian animal sculpture. Like the anthropomorphic images of divinity, those of the sacred bull are carved in many different styles but are primarily a contribution of the art of South India. The posture of these animal figures is usually the same: they recline in a slightly asymmetrical way, as if having just lowered themselves into this position, with their legs and tail tucked under and their head attentively raised in a noble attitude. Generally they were placed facing the sanctuary that held the main symbol of Shiva. Intricate garlands of jewelry, bells and other trappings, and linear accents enhance this monumental yet sensitively modeled animal manifestation of the presence of a god.

Navatmaka Heruka, INDIAN, FROM BIHAR, SENA DYNASTY, ABOUT TWELFTH CENTURY

BRONZE, ENCRUSTED WITH SILVER, HEIGHT 5½″
PURCHASED: JOSEPH E. TEMPLE FUND. 68-164-2

Images of Heruka are action symbols of Tantric Buddhism, a cult of ecstasy rich in esoteric cosmic and sexual imagery; as such, they may be seen to be complements of the serenity of the images of the Buddha. Here, Navatmaka Heruka—eight-faced (each three-eyed), sixteen-armed, and four-legged—dances in the ecstatic embrace of his partner Nairatma ("Selflessness"), symbolizing the rapture of attaining a state of selfless detachment. The two conjoined bodies are at the center of a magic space created by the radiating circle of Heruka's many arms and a garland of severed heads. A single mighty dome of flaming hair caps the eight wrathful faces of this vigorous, arrestingly complex image.

Khasarpana (Lokeshvara), INDIAN, FROM ORISSA, GANGA DYNASTY, TWELFTH CENTURY

INDURATED TALC, HEIGHT 31¾"
PURCHASED: JOSEPH E. TEMPLE FUND.
41-23-1

The Buddhist Lord of Mercy, Khasarpana, is one of the forms of the savior Avalokiteshvara. Like most Indian images, this is conceived for a shallow wall niche, as one of many collateral figures punctuating and giving expression to the temple architecture. The void between the trefoil arch of the throne and the divinity seated on a lotus suggests the interior of a mountain cave, where the god resides. The small figures set in profusion around the upper half of Khasarpana are the attributes of any image of divinity, whether Hindu or Buddhist, and include such symbols of sovereignty as the lion rampant over the elephant; the grotesque animal-legged, yet somewhat human, dwarfs; and the celestial figures hovering above them. However, to Khasarpana exclusively belong the four acolytes placed aside and below the lotus throne and also the demon Sucimukha ("Needlemouth"), who kneels near the god's right foot, anxious to sip if only one drop of the honey of mercy that flows from his right hand. The left hand, now broken, grasped the stalk of the lotus flower above, the symbol of Avalokiteshvara.

Pillared Temple Hall from Madura, South India, VIJAYANAGAR DYNASTY,
MID-SIXTEENTH CENTURY

GIVEN IN MEMORY OF ADELINE PEPPER GIBSON BY SUSAN PEPPER GIBSON,
MARY GIBSON HENRY, AND HENRY C. GIBSON. 19-714

Reconstructed from the ruins of several shrines from a temple compound devoted to worship of
the god Vishnu, this Hindu temple interior is the only example of Indian stone architecture in
an American museum. The monolithic, highly complex carved granite pillars are arranged to
form an intermediate temple hall, a space where pilgrims might prepare themselves for worship.
From the pillars project life-size figures of heroes, sages, and divine beings that worshipfully flank
the nave, which leads to the door to the innermost sanctuary, where the main image of the divinity
was located. Above, bracket capitals in the form of lions, dividing a series of narrative relief panels
showing episodes from an Indian epic, complete the sculptural articulation of the monumental,
shadowy interior.

Prince Manohar Receives a Magic Ring from a Wizard, INDIAN,
FROM DECCAN, 1742

ILLUMINATED MANUSCRIPT PAINTING, GOUACHE ON PAPER, 8¾ × 5⅝″
THE PHILIP S. COLLINS COLLECTION. 45-65-22

In the *Garden of Love,* an ancient Sanskrit romantic fairytale, Prince Manohar wanders from
land to land in search of Madhumalati, his love. Deep in a forest he finds a hermit who gives him
a magic ring for protection during his travels. Here, in an illustration from a unique Deccani-
Urdu version of this romance, the emaciated sage—entwined with serpents, haloed by birds,
surrounded by other actual and imaginary creatures, and set off by foliage against the flat darkness
of night—confronts the steadfast prince. Human figures in profile are as much a part of this style
of painting as are the profile views of tigers and monsters, showing partly Chinese ancestry as
well as traces of Western modeling, fully integrated into the eerie mood of the painting.

"*Dragon*" *Carpet*, CAUCASIAN,
LATE SEVENTEENTH CENTURY

WOOL, 17' × 7'10"
GIVEN IN MEMORY OF PHILIP M.
SHARPLES BY MEMBERS OF THE
SHARPLES FAMILY. 48-83-1

Thought to have been made in the southern
Caucasus in workshops that had produced carpets for Abbas the Great, Shah of Persia from
1587 to 1628, the seventeenth- and eighteenth-
century "dragon" carpets have been prized for
their clean, bold patterns of jagged bands, ornamental leaves, and complex palmette forms presented in a range of relatively few strong yet
harmonious colors. Dragon carpets take their
name from the stylized crested dragons that
appear in pairs flanking a rounded, diagonally
ornamented blossom, like supporters beside an
heraldic shield; in characteristic Chinese manner, they have flames at their shoulders and their
hips. This dragon carpet is the most spectacular
showpiece among the numerous carpets of this
type owned by museums in America and Europe.

Cloister from Saint-Genis-des-Fontaines, France, ABOUT 1160–1180

The Abbey of Saint-Genis-des-Fontaines in the French Pyrenees was founded by Benedictine monks in 819. Continually under attack by Saracens from Spain, it was destroyed several times before the mid-twelfth century, when it was rebuilt for the last time, incorporating elements of earlier structures. The abbey was abandoned just before the French Revolution. Its cloister was dismantled in 1925, and more than one-third of it was reassembled to form this cloister, which on a reduced scale evokes the tranquil, contemplative atmosphere that was at the heart of medieval monastic life. Among the carvings on the capitals—some of which may be from the same period as a lintel dated 1020–1021 that is still conserved in place on the abbey church—are such animals as a turtle, giraffe, and peacock; flowers; coats of arms; and scenes inspired by the Vision of the Apocalypse. The marble fountain, from the nearby Abbey of Saint-Michel-de-Cuxa, is ornamented with a columned arcade which seems to echo that of the cloister itself.

Holofernes' Army Crossing the Euphrates, FRENCH, 1246–1248

STAINED AND PAINTED GLASS, DIAMETER 26″
GIVEN BY MRS. CLEMENT BIDDLE WOOD. 30-24-3

This stained-glass panel originally formed part of the spectacular decoration of the Sainte-Chapelle in Paris, a royal chapel built by Saint Louis as a shrine for holy relics. Inside this outstanding monument of Gothic architecture, which has been preserved to this day, fifteen tall windows made up of numerous small panels showing Old and New Testament scenes fill the interior with an awesome multihued, jewel-like color. This panel, depicting Holofernes' army crossing the Euphrates, was part of the window with subjects from the Books of Judith and Job. It shows knights on horseback fording a river, according to the passage, "And [Holofernes] crossed the Euphrates and came into Mesopotamia" (Judith 2:14). Although delineated in a refined courtly style, the figures and gestures show striking foreshortening and freely drawn detail—some of which is purely fanciful, such as the emphatic eyebrows on the horses. The overall effect of strength is heightened by the bold pattern of the strong lead lines.

Jan van Eyck (FLEMISH, 1380/1400–1441)
Saint Francis Receiving the Stigmata

OIL ON PANEL, 4⅞ × 5¾"
JOHN G. JOHNSON COLLECTION. 314

According to the story of the Life of Saint Francis of Assisi, in 1224 he withdrew for prayer and fasting to Mount Alverno, accompanied by Brother Leo. There, in a mystical ecstasy, he saw the vision of a seraphim bearing a crucifix, with the wounds of Christ emanating rays that pierced the saint's body. It is a narrative full of visionary drama and expressive animation; yet in this devout Northern interpretation of the story (reproduced in its actual size) the figures have the immobility of a still life. Flowers, stratified rocks, and the distant town are all shown with the same impartial detail and objectivity as the mute face of the saint, passively receiving the stigmata while Brother Leo slumps, oblivious to the miraculous happening. A remarkably new attitude in the history of religious representation is apparent here: it conveys a new form of piety in which both the real and the supernatural are depicted with equal authority and refined illusionism— and hence equal conviction.

Giovanni di Paolo (ITALIAN, SIENESE, ABOUT 1403–1482)
The Miracle of Saint Nicolas of Tolentino, ABOUT 1456

OIL ON PANEL, 20½ × 16⅝"
JOHN G. JOHNSON COLLECTION. INV. 723

The paintings of Giovanni di Paolo, especially on this small and intimate scale, present a world of legendary narrative which is as much emotionally felt as rationally understood. The charming hillock waves marching tidily off to the horizon; the broken masts and sails decoratively strewn across the sky like a flight of swallows; the lurid temptress mermaid; the vision of the benign saint quelling the storm, sure and calm in the dark night—all these details have the beguiling super-reality of a fairytale. And it is through this suspension of the rules of nature that the artist has been able to make the event appear all the more miraculous. Giovanni di Paolo worked in Siena in the mid-fourteenth century and continued the lyrical, Late Gothic style that had dominated nearly all of Europe at the beginning of the century. His paintings are pervaded with the gentle transcendentalism and mysticism which so strongly characterize the art and thought of Siena.

35

Pietro Lorenzetti (ITALIAN, SIENESE, ACTIVE 1305–1348)
Virgin and Child Enthroned, ABOUT 1320–1329

OIL ON PANEL, 49⅝ × 29¾″
JOHN G. JOHNSON COLLECTION. 91

The subject of the enthroned Virgin with the Christ Child on her lap, first introduced into Italian painting during the late Middle Ages, is by its very nature symmetrical, hieratic, and severe—the perfect votive image for large altarpieces. At the beginning of the fourteenth century, with the Florentine master Giotto, followed in Siena by Pietro Lorenzetti, this treatment of the subject was infused with a new human vitality and warmth. The Virgin sits in monumental splendor on her inlaid throne, and her musing, unfocused gaze completes the impression of a regal, somewhat remote presence. However, the Child, with momentary animation, raises His right hand in blessing and opens His left in a gesture of embrace, directed to the small figure of an adoring monk who undoubtedly commissioned this painting. The inclusion of a mortal before the heavenly throne introduces a narrative and temporal element into this dignified, powerful image.

Desiderio da Settignano (ITALIAN, FLORENTINE, 1428–1464)

Virgin and Child, ABOUT 1460

MARBLE, 23¼ × 16¾"
PURCHASED: THE W. P. WILSTACH COLLECTION. W 30-1-2

This carving of the Virgin and Child is said to be from the Hospital of Santa Maria Nuova in Florence, where it may have adorned a small chapel. Desiderio da Settignano was known for his reliefs and busts of smiling young women and children, and his tender, lyrical approach can best be seen in a group of his Madonna reliefs. The Virgin is interpreted here in the humanizing Renaissance spirit as a smiling young mother playing with her child, and only the haloes identify them as holy figures. Their youth and freshness are enhanced by the smooth finish of the delicately shaded marble. Even in his lifetime Desiderio was famous for his beautifully subtle technique of low relief. An extraordinary effect of distance is achieved by the many, minutely varied levels of carving. The angels in the background have the delicacy of a drawing, while the hands and faces of the foreground figures stand out more boldly in comparatively high relief—and all achieved in less than one inch of actual depth.

Rogier van der Weyden (FLEMISH, ABOUT 1399–1464)

Crucifixion with the Virgin and Saint John, ABOUT 1450–1460

OIL ON TWO PANELS, EACH 71 × 36⅜″
JOHN G. JOHNSON COLLECTION. 334, 335

It is known from certain fifteenth-century manuscript illuminations that as part of the embellishment of the church during specific periods of the religious calendar a red drape was hung at the end of the nave behind the crucifix. This simple yet emphatic idea has been adapted by Rogier van der Weyden in these monumental panels. The figures are essentially sculpture transformed into painting, and even the crisp folds of the resplendent scarlet hangings have been retained. In a shallow space blocked by an abrupt wall, the Virgin swoons into the arms of Saint John at the sight of her executed son. The emotional intensity of the two mourners is compressed to a level of timeless tragedy. Their pathos is real and deeply felt, yet the drama is detached from everyday reality: the sky is a flat field of gold and the figures are transformed into austere, regal symbols.

Benedict Master (GERMAN, ACTIVE 1510–1515)

Education of the Virgin, ABOUT 1510

POLYCHROME AND GILDED WOOD, HEIGHT 26⅜"
GIVEN BY ELIZABETH MALCOLM BOWMAN IN MEMORY OF
WENDELL PHILLIPS BOWMAN. 30·1·163

The story of the Life of the Virgin was frequently retold in medieval miracle plays, whose elaborate productions are known to have served as models for painters and sculptors. Realistic, even humorous episodes from the secular world were included in these dramatizations of sacred stories, just as acutely observed details from daily life were introduced into this religious group. Saint Anne, wearing a housewifely kerchief, gently instructs her daughter, the Virgin, whose dress is elegant and, especially the sleeves, in the height of fashion. However the symbolic attributes associated with these personages have not been forgotten: the mother is clothed in a red dress and a green mantle, while the Virgin wears a crown and a cloak of blue. The realism of the costumes gives way at the hems to an exuberant animation, a witness to the virtuosity of the anonymous master from the Hildesheim region who carved this splendid Late Gothic sculpture.

Cabinet, FRENCH, LATE SIXTEENTH CENTURY

WALNUT, HEIGHT 75 ¼"
GIVEN BY CHESTER W. LARNER. 30·1·181

This ornate Burgundian Renaissance cabinet, with its brilliantly carved figures and architectural motifs, would surely have been outstanding even in an equally opulent room of sixteenth-century France. The plain arches in each panel (the only elements not embellished with carving) were probably painted with gilded or monochrome figures, simulating sculpture in a niche, just as much of the cabinet was once decorated with gilding and painting. The bizarre half-human figures and the crisply chiseled moldings, the human and animal masks, and the garlands of fruit are forms borrowed from the Italian Renaissance and ultimately derived from Greek and Roman examples. These elements were illustrated in the numerous patternbooks widely used during this period. One such book was published in 1572 by the Dijon master Hughes Sambin, whose style is closely related to that of the carving of this piece. The plates of his book were sources for many furniture carvers and may well have inspired the decoration of this luxurious cabinet.

Luca della Robbia (ITALIAN, FLORENTINE, 1400–1482)
and Andrea della Robbia (ITALIAN, FLORENTINE, 1435–1525)

Virgin and Child

GLAZED TERRA-COTTA, DIAMETER 65¾″
PURCHASED: THE W. P. WILSTACH COLLECTION. 30-1-64

Luca della Robbia achieved great fame by perfecting a method of making polychrome sculpture from glazed terra-cotta, in strong and pure colors of lasting quality well suited to exterior architectural embellishment. He traveled as far as Spain and France to satisfy the growing demand for his sculpture and headed a large workshop that included his nephew and great-nephews, who continued this work after his death. In this large circular relief of the Virgin and Child, probably from the Alberti Palace in Florence, Luca uses color only to make the pure white figures stand out against the rich blue background; the background is plain but for the ethereal rays, which may at one time have been painted with gold, and the angels bearing a scroll proclaiming "Gloria in excelsis Deo." In contrast, a sumptuous richness is achieved by the variety of color and form in the formalized garland of fruit and flowers said to have been modeled by Luca's nephew Andrea.

41

Master E. S. (GERMAN, ACTIVE ABOUT 1450–1467/68)

Emperor Augustus and the Tiburtine Sibyl, ABOUT 1466

ENGRAVING, 8⅝ × 5⅝″
PURCHASED IN HONOR OF LESSING J. ROSENWALD'S EIGHTIETH BIRTHDAY
WITH FUNDS GIVEN BY JULIUS ROSENWALD II, LESSING J. ROSENWALD,
AND OTHERS, SUPPLEMENTED BY THE LOLA DOWNIN PECK FUND. 71-29-1

Prints by the unidentified German engraver known as Master E. S. are extremely rare and precious. As here, his work is generally unsigned, but some three hundred engravings have been attributed to him, based on comparison with eighteen known engravings signed with the monogram "E.S." The subject of this print is an apocryphal story that had become popularized through one of the most famous books of the late Middle Ages, *The Golden Legend* of Jacobus de Voragine, and through popular prints. It was said that the Roman Senate wished to deify Emperor Augustus, who took the precaution, however, of asking the Tiburtine Sibyl if there would ever appear a more important person than he. At this moment the Virgin appeared holding the Christ Child, and the Sibyl said to Augustus, "This child will be greater than thou." The celestial apparition of the Virgin and Child is shown through a window at the upper right.

Choir Screen from the Chapel of the Château of Pagny, near Dijon, France
ABOUT 1535–1540

GIVEN BY ELI KIRK PRICE. 30-1-84

In the sixteenth century, the illustrious Admiral of France Philippe Chabot transformed much of his château at Pagny according to the taste of the Italian Renaissance, which was then dominant at the French court of Francis I. As part of his program of embellishment, Chabot added this varicolored-marble and alabaster choir screen to the château's Gothic chapel. The screen is still Gothic in contour—a crucifix originally surmounted the central column and extended high into the Gothic ribbed vaulting; the four alabaster statues (a bishop, the Virgin, Saint John, and a prophet) function as the customary Gothic pinnacles—but the ornament is totally Renaissance in spirit. Columns, arches, and pilasters, ornamental figures and cherubs bearing garlands—all are based on classical models as interpreted by Italian Renaissance artists. In the frieze above the central arch, carved in high relief, are the coats of arms of Chabot, his wife, and her uncle Cardinal de Givry (surmounted by his Cardinal's hat) and the dates 1536 and 1538. The carved and painted altarpiece behind the screen, also from the chapel at Pagny, was made in Antwerp about 1530.

Armorial Carpet, SPANISH, FIRST HALF OF THE FIFTEENTH CENTURY

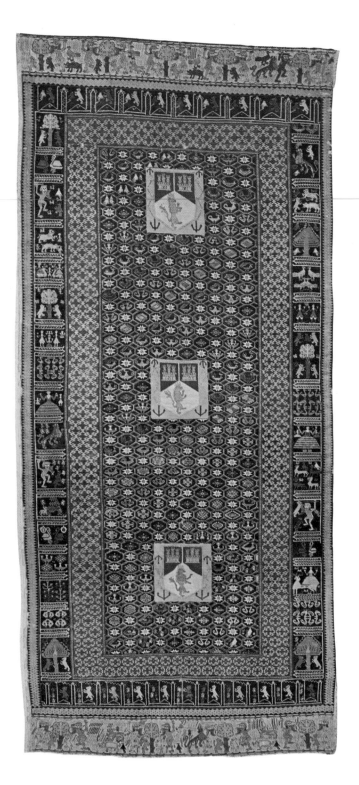

WOOL, 19′5½″ × 8′9½″
JOSEPH LEES WILLIAMS MEMORIAL
COLLECTION. 55-65-21

Shortly after the art of making twisted-pile carpets was introduced into Spain by the Moors, the
weaving of this armorial carpet was undertaken,
probably for the founder of the royal house of
Castile, Fadrique Enriquez, Lord of Medina and
Admiral of Castile, the grandfather of King
Ferdinand of Spain. His coat of arms, an upright
lion with two triple-towered castles above, bor-
dered by anchors and ropes (the insignia of the
admiralship of Castile), is repeated three times
in the center field. The motifs within the central
allover pattern of octagons, the wide side border,
and the unusual extra border at each end include
strange trees, stylized half-human figures, sav-
ages with shields hunting bears, and—perhaps
most curious of all—ladies wearing crinoline-like
skirts, some riding camels. A decorative pattern
in the main border at each end, formed by the
Cufic inscription *La ilah ill Allah* ("There is no
God but Allah"), indicates its Moorish workmanship.

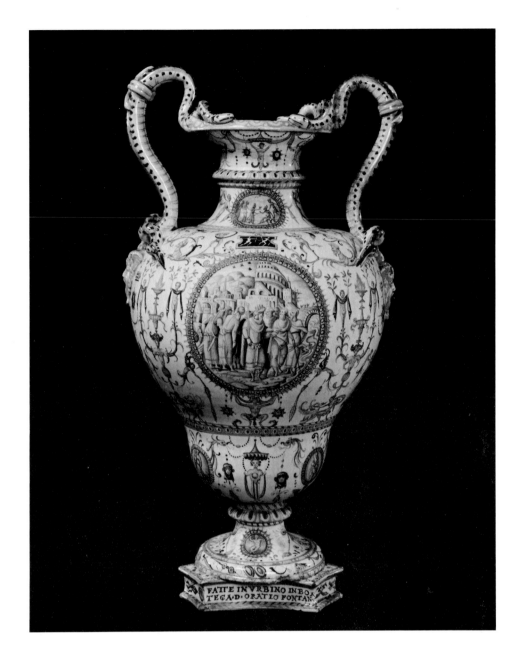

Vase, ITALIAN, 1565–1575

MAJOLICA (TIN-GLAZED POTTERY), HEIGHT 21¼"
PURCHASED: BLOOMFIELD MOORE AND MISCELLANEOUS FUNDS. 44-15-2

Majolica from the workshop of Orazio Fontana in Urbino—the makers of this urn according to the inscription on the base—was prized throughout Europe during the Renaissance for its brilliant colors and pure white background. The monochrome narrative panels of this urn and its companion piece in the Museum (perhaps once part of an extensive table service) illustrate scenes from the Old Testament. Here in the large central scene the building of the Temple of Solomon has been represented, with the half-built structure in the distance and King Solomon, wearing his crown, explaining his plans in the foreground. The elaboration of the entire surface follows ancient Roman precedents. The small medallions are modeled after Roman gems or medals and the grotesques (imaginary figures, part-human, part-animal, interwoven with plant forms) are derived from the decoration of Roman grottoes, which was newly discovered in the Renaissance and soon popularized by Raphael and sixteenth-century patternbooks.

Nicolas Poussin (FRENCH, 1594–1665)
The Birth of Venus, ABOUT 1635

OIL ON CANVAS, 45¼ × 58″
PURCHASED: THE GEORGE W. ELKINS COLLECTION. E 32-1-1

The scene is all triumph and pageantry. Venus glides across the sea with her full entourage of dolphins, maidens, and rosy children strewing flowers, while the adoring Neptune reins in next to her with his sea horses, heralded by trumpet-blaring Tritons. Gods and goddesses perform for us in a tableau which is one of the most complex yet graceful compositions to come down from the seventeenth century. Poussin has often been called a "classicist," a master of equilibrium and serenity—and never more apparent than here. He had an incomparable genius for depicting sensuous beauty and placing it on a plane of contemplative pleasure, a rare gift seldom equaled in the history of Western painting. It is not surprising then that this picture, one of the most perfect examples of his genius, has had a most illustrious history. Commissioned by Cardinal Richelieu, it eventually passed to the Russian imperial court in the collection of Catherine the Great. It remained in Russia until 1932, when it was purchased from the Soviet government for this Museum.

Peter Paul Rubens (FLEMISH, 1577–1640)

Prometheus Bound, ABOUT 1611–1612

OIL ON CANVAS, 95⅝ × 82½"
PURCHASED: THE W. P. WILSTACH COLLECTION. W 50-3-1

When Rubens painted this picture shortly after his return from Italy in 1608, he was fully aware of the potency of the Greek myth of Prometheus, the god who stole the life-sustaining fire from Olympus and gave it to mankind. For this transgression Zeus had him chained to a rock in the Caucasus Mountains, and each day an eagle devoured his liver, only to have it grow back again every night. Prometheus has been seen as the paragon of the hero, the defiant champion of mankind who is left to struggle eternally against his fate. This depiction of the male nude enduring the cutting talons and beak of the giant bird is one of the most jarring, emotionally effective interpretations of the theme. The writhing torso of the hero and the frenzied, flapping bird communicate the horrifying incident in the most immediate way. Yet it is much more than a scene of torture. The colossal scale and muscularity of the figure, the majesty of the eagle, and the stormy sky leave no doubt that this is the torment of a god and an enduring image of a hero.

47

Room from Het Scheepje ("The Little Boat"), Haarlem, 1608

GIVEN BY EDWARD BOK. 28-66-1

At the beginning of the seventeenth century, a young Dutch sailor, Dirk Dirick, gave up the seaman's life and settled in Haarlem, where he became a prosperous brewer and amassed substantial property. In 1608 he built a house that he called Het Scheepje ("The Little Boat"), which originally included this room, one of the finest secular rooms of the period still in existence. Quite small in size and resembling the immaculate interiors depicted by Vermeer and other Dutch painters, it was used for living, cooking, and sleeping as well (a bed is built into an alcove and hidden by a curtain). It was not lack of means but, rather, the frugality of Dutch burgher life which demanded that this one room serve so many functions. Yet such a small space has been given great style and an imposing effect by the elaborate fireplace, with its carved sandstone columns, delftware tile backing, and finely carved mantel, and by its handsome furnishings— brass, copper, and pewter utensils, delft plates, and an Eastern rug on the table. On the left wall are a heavily carved oak cabinet, called a *Beeldenkast*, and a linenpress, in which damp linen was placed to be flattened.

Jan Steen (DUTCH, 1626–1679)

Moses Striking the Rock

OIL ON CANVAS, 37¾ × 39½"
JOHN G. JOHNSON COLLECTION. 509

Jan Steen found a ready market among his burgher compatriots for his figure-packed depictions—
often rowdy and humorous—of taverns and brothels. He brought to this genre a sympathetic
warmth and comic observation that have survived the context of his time and continue to amuse
and beguile. Even in his religious subjects he rarely adjusted his style away from genre to a more
elevated, nonworldly plane. If anything, the throng of Israelites here, rejoicing and partaking of
the spring that miraculously gushed forth in the desert when Moses struck the rock of Horeb,
seems to have presented a renewed challenge for the Dutch artist to depict as many emotions and
anecdotal details as possible. The wealth of characterizations here is truly Chaucerian: the thankful
and almost operatically pompous Moses, the wonderstruck boy who catches our gaze, the bacchantic
rowdy on the right, the elegant woman in court finery.

49

Georg Petel (GERMAN, 1590/93–1634)
Massacre of the Innocents

BRONZE, HEIGHT 17¾″
PURCHASED: FISKE AND MARIE KIMBALL
FUND. 69-40-1

The emotional extremes of this horrifying subject—Herod's decree that his soldiers slaughter
all the children of Bethlehem, to ensure the death
of the Christ Child—have caught the imagination of this Northern sculptor. The group he
modeled is visually complex, meant to be seen
from many viewpoints. With each new angle,
the viewer grasps more and more fully the
intricacy of the conception and the impact of the
figures. The exaggerated treatment of the veins
standing out on the muscular arms and the
rough texture of the drapery against the agitated
highlights of the flesh, which reveal the skillful
hand of the artist, give stunning conviction and
immediacy to the event as, with a cry, the
mother desperately tries to restrain the arm that
threatens yet another child while one already
lies dead at her feet.

The Battle of the Milvian Bridge, FRENCH, EARLY SEVENTEENTH CENTURY

TAPESTRY, WOOL, SILK, GOLD, AND SILVER, 15′11″ × 24′5″
GIVEN BY THE SAMUEL H. KRESS FOUNDATION. 59-78-3

In 1625, to commemorate the state visit to Paris of Cardinal Francesco Barberini, King Louis XIII presented the Cardinal with this tapestry and six others designed by the Flemish painter Peter Paul Rubens. Woven in the Saint-Marcel tapestry workshop in Paris, the series depicts events in the life of Constantine the Great, the first Christian Roman emperor. Here, Constantine's decisive victory over Maxentius at the Milvian Bridge in Rome (A.D. 312) is represented, a victory that was to make him sole emperor of the West. Constantine's army advances on the bridge, while Maxentius's men and horses are hurled into the river as the span collapses. In the foreground, Maxentius, crowned with a laurel wreath, still clutches his sword as he falls backward. Upon Cardinal Barberini's return to Italy, he commissioned Pietro da Cortona to design additional scenes for the series, which were woven in the tapestry workshop he established in Rome. This grand series of tapestries was probably reserved for important events and hung only on occasions of great ceremony in the Barberini Palace. Later dispersed, thirteen of the tapestries have only recently been reassembled and exhibited as an ensemble in the Great Hall of the Museum.

Francisco de Zurbarán (SPANISH, 1598–1664)
The Annunciation, 1650

OIL ON CANVAS, 7′1⅝″ × 10′4½″
PURCHASED: THE W. P. WILSTACH COLLECTION. W 00-1-16

Zurbarán was a native of Andalusia, where he spent much of his early career working on large narrative commissions for the numerous monastic orders of southern Spain. Upon his emergence as a mature artist in the 1630s, he had completely absorbed the Andalusian tradition of simplicity and unaffected realism, and achieved a style of virile, sober force. Generally working on a large scale against a dark background, he developed a technique of showing objects and figures in a strongly lighted, deeply shadowed space, which in satisfying the Counter-Reformation taste of his patrons served as an immediate and intense witness to the religious narrative or miracle depicted. Here, Gabriel appears to the Virgin in a drama of spare understatement in which the greatest animation is reserved for the jolly angels floating in a pink-orange haze that emanates from the Dove.

François-Thomas Germain (FRENCH, 1726–1791)
Tureen with Cover and Tray, 1759

SILVER GILT, HEIGHT 17″ (INCLUDING TRAY)
PURCHASED. 54-81-1a, b, c

As a third-generation Parisian silversmith, François-Thomas Germain inherited not only his family's tradition of consummate craftsmanship but also an established patronage among the most important royal houses in Europe. He designed for the courts of Russia and Portugal two very similar extravagant silver table services, each with almost three hundred pieces, including eight splendid tureens. This tureen bears the French marks of its maker, city, and date (F.T. Germain, Paris, 1759), as well as the Russian imperial coat of arms, modeled on each side of the body, and Russian marks recording the city and date of importation (St. Petersburg, 1762). It was originally ordered by Empress Elizabeth of Russia in 1756 as part of what was called the "Parisian Service," but was delivered only in 1767 (five years after Elizabeth's death) to her successor Catherine the Great. Germain enriched the curving forms of tureen and stand with splendidly modeled figures—satyrs, cherubs, and falcons—in a Rococo design elaborate enough to suit even the most luxurious tastes of his imperial patron.

Jean-Claude Duplessis (FRENCH, ACTIVE 1745–1774)

Sèvres Vase, 1753

SOFT-PASTE PORCELAIN, HEIGHT 9⅞″ (WITH LATER MOUNT)
BEQUEST OF ELEANORE ELKINS RICE. 39-41-56a

In 1753, encouraged by its patrons King Louis XV and Mme de Pompadour, the French national porcelain manufactory was authorized to move from Vincennes to larger quarters at Sèvres. That same year Jean-Claude Duplessis modeled this vase (one of a pair), a fact known from the date letter *A* marked on the bottom and from an original plaster model, similarly decorated with cherubs, still preserved in the Sèvres archives. Since 1745 Duplessis, as Goldsmith to the King, had supervised all modeling done at the factory as well as the production there of gilt-bronze mounts for porcelains. While vases for natural or porcelain flowers were standard Sèvres products, Duplessis furnished this one with the factory's latest innovation—the celebrated turquoise-blue glaze (*bleu céleste*), first used commercially in 1753. Similarly, he introduced a new form for the vase, with lobed trumpet mouth and foliate-scroll handles—a form that became so identified with its designer that it was known in factory records as a "Vase Duplessis."

Giovanni Battista Tiepolo (ITALIAN, VENETIAN, 1696–1770)

Venus and Vulcan

OIL ON CANVAS, 27 ⅛ × 34 ¼"
JOHN G. JOHNSON COLLECTION. 287

Giovanni Battista Tiepolo was the last great exponent of the tradition of Venetian painting and perhaps the greatest European painter of the eighteenth century. He was the creator of vast decorative and religious scenes of astonishing invention and drama as well as innumerable smaller oil paintings and drawings, admired as much for their concise characterization of subject as for their brilliant, assured technique. Here, Venus, the wife of Vulcan, master armorer of the gods, has returned to the cave-forge of her husband. In her seductive fashion, she induces him to make the arms necessary for the eventual triumph of her son Aeneas in the founding of Rome. The dark, flame-lit chamber with its brawny laborers, especially the lame and rustic god, stands in startling contrast to the radiant, haughty beauty of Venus and her entourage, who have been wafted in on an unsoiled cloud. It is a picture which is at once myth, gossip, splendid decoration, and—with a slightly bitter bias—a telling statement on social mores and the human comedy.

Claude Michel, known as Clodion
(FRENCH, 1734–1814)
Dancing Nymphs, LATE EIGHTEENTH CENTURY

PLASTER, HEIGHT 89 ½″ (WITHOUT BASE)
GIVEN BY EVA ROBERTS STOTESBURY
IN MEMORY OF EDWARD T.
STOTESBURY. 38-24-7

These dancing maidens, a slight breeze animating the draperies suggestively clinging to their bodies, once decorated the circular dining room of a fashionable townhouse on the Rue des Petites Ecuries in Paris. With three similar groups (a second also in the Museum, the two others now in the Musée des Arts Décoratifs in Paris) they were the major decorative elements among the mirrors, columns, and niches in this elegant late-eighteenth-century interior. Although then in the midst of a classical revival, French art had not lost its taste for playfulness and charm. Clodion, one of the most popular sculptors of his time, added to these mythological figures a lightness and grace not to be found in the Roman forms on which they were based. Famous for his small terra-cotta figures, he continued to delight in intricacies of detail even when working in plaster on a large scale. Here Clodion has produced a work of great monumentality, yet the near life-size figures appear to turn lightly, with their fingertips scarcely touching the weighty bowl of fruit.

Salon from the Hôtel Letellier, Paris, 1789

GIVEN BY ELEANORE ELKINS RICE. 28-52-1

The house at 13 Rue Royale in Paris, the Hôtel Letellier, from which this salon comes, is known by the name of its architect and first owner. Begun by Louis Letellier in 1781, it must have been virtually complete by February 1783, when a contract was signed with the firm of Pierre Fixon to decorate the interior with sculptured ornaments, including five large cast-plaster reliefs for the overdoors of the salon. These decorations were executed between March and July of 1789—the dates known from original inscriptions found behind the paneling when the room was dismantled for shipment to the United States in 1928. Classical architectural details and sculptural motifs such as the Nereids supporting urns are characteristic of the refined, Greek- and Roman-inspired decorative vocabulary popular in France from the 1750s. This was an elegant style destined to be altered by the events of the French Revolution, which began with the fall of the Bastille less than a fortnight after the completion of this salon.

Room from Wrightington Hall, near Wigan, Lancashire, England, 1748

During the mid-eighteenth century, the great Elizabethan house Wrightington Hall was enlarged with a new wing, which included this room. The floral garlands and shellwork carved on the mantel and overmantel were inspired by the fashionable decorative repertory of the Continental Rococo style, which was given both Chinese and Gothic accents by English cabinetmakers. The mahogany commode from Raynham Hall, Norfolk, decorated with sprays of flowers similar to those of the architectural decoration, was designed by Thomas Chippendale and published in his *Gentleman and Cabinetmaker's Director*. The elaborate candlestand with stalactites, dolphins, and naturalistic boughs closely follows one published by the cabinetmaker Thomas Johnson in 1758, and the same exotic taste is apparent in the windmill girandole, a candleholder, also credited to Johnson. Over the mantel hangs the portrait of *Master Bunbury* by Sir Joshua Reynolds, exhibited at the Royal Academy in London in 1781. Painted about five years later, George Romney's sketch of *Lady Hamilton as Miranda*, seen at the left, is an important study for a lost "Tempest" composition commissioned by Josiah Boydell as part of a series illustrating the works of Shakespeare.

William Blake (ENGLISH, 1757–1827)
The Death of Ezekiel's Wife, 1785–1786

PENCIL, PEN, AND WASH ON PAPER, 13 5/8 × 18 7/8″
GIVEN BY MRS. WILLIAM T. TONNER. 64-110-11

The visionary imagination of William Blake found expression both in mystical poetry and in engraving, drawing, and watercolor painting of exquisite refinement. With affecting simplicity and sublime feeling, he interwove lyric verse and fantastic illustrations in numerous works ranging in subject from Virgil and the Bible to Chaucer and Dante. Divine love and sympathy, self-sacrifice and forgiveness—these are some of the recurring Christian themes of Blake's verbal and visual lyricism. This watercolor shows the prophet Ezekiel, who having preached one morning of God's command neither to weep nor to mourn for the dead was challenged by Jehovah that same evening to follow his own precept when his wife died. Mourners surround his wife's bier with bowed heads and grief-stricken gestures, while Ezekiel kneels apart, facing the viewer in an attitude of emotional restraint and self-control. From this Old Testament episode of stoical suffering, Blake has created a powerful and comforting spiritual statement.

Drawing Room from Lansdowne House, London, 1765–1773

In 1761 the Earl of Bute, prime minister in the reign of George III, commissioned the architect Robert Adam to design a townhouse on Berkeley Square in London. While the house was under construction its title shifted to the Earl of Shelbourne, later the Marquess of Lansdowne, but the building continued as planned. By the early 1770s the decoration of the major rooms was complete. According to the contract for this room—the first drawing room—G. B. Cipriani was employed to paint scenes from antiquity and Antonio Zucchi to add the ornamental designs derived from Roman frescoes, both artists working within Adam's overall scheme. The room stands as a prime example of Adam's clear and articulate classical style. As now installed with Benjamin West's heroic neoclassical painting *Agrippina with the Ashes of Germanicus* (1770) above the fireplace and Cipriani's four overdoors illustrating the Education of Achilles, this interior represents English progressive taste at its best just before the American Revolution. The suite of furniture was supplied by Samuel Fell and William Turton in 1771 for Moor Park, a house in Hertfordshire, and the carpet was woven at Axminster, probably in the 1770s. (*See also Cover.*)

Benjamin West (AMERICAN, 1738–1820)

Benjamin Franklin Drawing Electricity from the Sky, 1805

OIL ON PAPER ON CANVAS, 12¼ × 10″
GIVEN BY MR. AND MRS. WHARTON SINKLER. 58-132-1

Benjamin West has chosen the most dramatic event from Franklin's life to portray the qualities of a hero in the midst of discovery. Painted at least fifteen years after Franklin's death, the picture is not so much a record of the features of the great statesman-inventor as a memorial to his fame. West has altered the facts of history to serve his artistic ends. Franklin is depicted as the dignified elder statesman who exists in the public memory, rather than as the man of forty-six who proved that lightning is a form of static electricity. Instead of re-creating a specific landscape, West has set the scene in the heart of a storm and portrayed Franklin's assistants as a team of cherubs. Amid the violent tempest, dramatized by his billowing cloak and tossing locks, Franklin's scientific curiosity is transformed into heroic concentration as he gazes at the spark that jumps to his hand.

Charles Willson Peale (AMERICAN, 1741–1827)
The Staircase Group, 1795

OIL ON CANVAS, WITH WOODEN FRAME
AND STEP, 94 ½ × 47″
THE GEORGE W. ELKINS COLLECTION.
E 45-1-1

In Charles Willson Peale's *Staircase Group*, the directness of observation that defines Peale's best portrait style is carried beyond portraiture to the point of pleasurable deception. As the young men—Titian Ramsey and Raphaelle Peale, two of the artist's sons—turn to look back through the doorway, they appear for a moment to exist in the viewer's own space and time. The pose of life-size figures in action, the carefully studied play of light and shadow, and the meticulous rendering of detail combine to create this startling illusion, and Peale enhanced it by placing the painting within a door frame and adding a wooden step that projects into the room. Another of his sons, Rembrandt Peale, remembered that George Washington, on a visit to Peale's museum, bowed to the painted figures as he passed. *The Staircase Group* is first mentioned in 1795, in the exhibition catalogue of the Columbianum, the Philadelphia art academy that Peale had helped to organize. At this time, he had turned his attention from painting to the organization of his museum and the study of natural sciences, so it is likely that *The Staircase Group* was made expressly for public exhibition, to serve as a vivid reminder of Peale's great skill as an artist.

William Rush (AMERICAN, 1756–1833)
The Schuylkill Freed, 1828

PINE, ORIGINALLY PAINTED, LENGTH 86½″
ON DEPOSIT FROM THE COMMISSIONERS OF FAIRMOUNT PARK

As well as providing an improved water supply for the city, the waterworks begun in 1811 at Fairmount in Philadelphia was designed as a public garden, and the elevated site, with its reservoir where the Philadelphia Museum of Art now stands, its picturesque buildings, and its views of the river, soon became a showplace. To adorn the buildings that housed the pumping machinery at riverside, William Rush carved two allegorical figures representing the Schuylkill River and the waterworks. A reclining male figure, *The Schuylkill Chained*, depicts the river controlled as a source of power. According to a contemporary description the matching female figure, *The Schuylkill Freed*, "is represented as seated near the pump which pours water into the reservoir. On the left side is represented a water-wheel; her left arm gently waved over it is indicative of the water-power; her right arm or elbow rests on the edge of a large vase, representing the reservoir at Fairmount. On the side of the vase a pipe represents the ascending main. Water gushes out of the top, falling into the vase, and, to make it more picturesque, but not appropriate, overflowing the vase and falling down its sides."

Drawing Room from the Samuel Powel House, Philadelphia, ABOUT 1772

GIVEN BY MR. AND MRS. WOLF KLEBASKY (25-61-1), GEORGE D. WIDENER (26-41-1), AND H. LOUIS DUHRING (26-54-1, 27-76-1)

Samuel Powel—merchant, land speculator, and Mayor of Philadelphia from 1775 to 1789—purchased his house at 244 South Third Street on August 2, 1769. Entries in his ledger show that **by** November of that year he had commissioned architect Robert Smith to finish one room and make alterations in another; and that Barnard and Jugiez were paid for carving and Timothy Berrett for "painting and bordering." The architectural decoration of this room, originally located at the second-floor front, combines in a symmetrical plan the classical vocabulary of broken pediments and fluted pilasters, familiar in English house design, with the flamboyant, asymmetrical plaster ornamentation derived from the French Rococo style. Powel's Queen Anne style armchair had been made before 1760 in the earlier expression of the Rococo style for which Philadelphia chairmakers were deservedly famous. The taste of the Philadelphia gentleman was well served by skilled local craftsmen, among them clockmakers, cabinetmakers, and silversmiths, while the English paintings, Oriental porcelain garniture on the mantel, and crystal chandelier would have been supplied by Philadelphia's rich mercantile trade.

Colonial Costumes

SATIN DRESS, AMERICAN, 1778
GIVEN BY MRS. J. BUNFORD SAMUEL. 08-237

EMBROIDERED VELVET SUIT, FRENCH, ABOUT 1770
GIVEN BY CHARLES F. SAAKE. 53-13-1

These stylish costumes, worn in colonial America, reflect the widespread influence of French court elegance on fashionable taste. In the French-style dress of satin brocade in large floral and ribbon design, Rebecca Machado attended the Mischianza Ball, the infamous farewell banquet given in Philadelphia on May 18, 1778, to honor Sir William Howe, then commander-in-chief of the British armies in America. The closely fitted bodice, with a square neckline, is fastened in front by a series of bows arranged in ladder-like fashion (*échelle*); the divided skirt is draped at the sides to form panniers and reveal an underskirt of the same material. The gentleman's elaborate costume, of a type referred to as "habit à la française," was designed for formal functions. All edges of the rich velvet coat—the high standing collar, curved pockets with flaps, and cuffs—are lavishly embroidered in a floral design worked in subtle pastel shades.

Thomas Tucker (AMERICAN, 1812–1890)

Vase, ABOUT 1835

HARD-PASTE PORCELAIN, HEIGHT 20¾″
PURCHASED: JOSEPH E. TEMPLE FUND. 16-185

Earlier attempts at porcelain manufacture had been made in Philadelphia, but it was only in the
1820s with the efforts of William Ellis Tucker, who initiated experiments in the backyard of his
father's Market Street china shop, that a successful enterprise was begun. The factory was in
operation from 1825 to 1852 (production having been continued after William's death in 1831
by his brother Thomas), producing a true and high-quality ware. With fashionable French porcelains from Sèvres and Nast as their models, the Tuckers shaped and painted a variety of pieces for
Philadelphia's eager clientele. In this vase, one of a pair considered the culmination of the factory's
achievement, Thomas Tucker has emulated the high style of foreign manufacture, creating an
appealing version of a French neoclassical form. The vases are fitted with fine ormolu handles in
the form of eagles with scrolled wings, designed by Friederich Sachse and cast by C. Cornelius &
Son of Philadelphia.

John Hewson (AMERICAN, BORN ENGLAND, 1744–1821)

Bedspread, LATE EIGHTEENTH CENTURY

PRINTED PLAIN-COTTON CLOTH, 8′6¾″ × 8′9¼″
GIVEN BY JOSEPH B. HODGSON, JR. 30-100-1

This bedspread, one of the finest known examples of early calico printing in America, was block printed by John Hewson, the first recorded calico printer in Pennsylvania. Born in 1744, he had been employed at Bromley Hall, near London, one of the most important factories and bleachyards in England. Hewson came to Philadelphia highly recommended with letters of introduction from Benjamin Franklin (who was then living in England) and worked in Kensington, on the outskirts of Philadelphia, from 1774 to 1810. Martha Washington came to inspect Hewson's printworks in 1775, and she is known to have worn dresses made of his calico fabric. This spread is block printed on cream-colored cotton in shades of brown and red, with the foliage in blue. The corners of each of the three borders are printed from separate blocks, a mark of the professional printer; the outer border is edged with simulated fringe and tassels.

Kitchen-Living Room from the House of the Miller at Millbach, Lebanon County, Pennsylvania, 1752

GIVEN BY MR. AND MRS. PIERRE S. DUPONT AND MR. AND MRS. LAMMOT DUPONT. 26-74-1

In 1752, Jerg Muller, a prosperous Pennsylvania miller, and his wife, Maria Caterina Muller, built a large stone house at Millbach, a predominantly German settlement in the Mill Run Valley of Lebanon County. The furniture, implements, and ceramics exhibited in his living room-kitchen reflect the success of endeavors such as his as well as the natural abundance of Pennsylvania "up-country." Bold, solid-hewn beams, carved door panels, and baroque architectural moldings, worked by the housewright, were as Germanic as the furniture created by the turner and the joiner. Under the valley's fertile farming soil lay a heavy red clay, which skilled native potters mined and molded, turned, and threw into an abundant variety of forms. Redware, decorated with colorful tulips, birds, fanciful flowers, and dancing figures in slip and sgraffito techniques, carried the traditions of the Old World to the New. Utilitarian implements, forged and wrought in iron and steel, furnish the great multipurpose fireplace, illustrating an imaginative self-sufficiency typical of the eighteenth-century household.

Sampler, AMERICAN, 1797

SILK ON CANVAS, 18 × 21½"
THE WHITMAN SAMPLER COLLECTION. 69-288-18

The making of samplers—the term is derived from the Latin *exemplar*, meaning "model"—
enjoyed great popularity throughout England and the Continent as early as the sixteenth century.
At first samplers were worked at random as a record of favorite motifs and stitches; later they
were made according to a formal scheme and as a basic part of every young woman's education.
Stitched predominantly in pink, green, and white with a black ground, this American sampler is
one of the few known having the canvas completely covered with needlework. "Wrought" by
Mary Wiggin in the year 1797, the embroidery shows three alphabets, the Tree of Life, lambs,
stylized flowers, an attractive symmetrical border, and a moralizing verse that reads: "Remark
this truth/ Enough to know/ Virtue in youth/ Is Bliss below/ Seek Virtue and of that possesst,/
To Providence resign the rest."

Shaker Furnishings, NINETEENTH CENTURY

GIVEN BY MR. AND MRS. JULIUS ZIEGET. 63-160

One manifestation of the prayer ritual of the Shakers was a "shaking," often accompanied by singing and motion in which the participants were "swiftly passing and repassing one another like clouds agitated by a mighty wind." Yet total restraint characterizes the utilitarian forms they produced and the organized routine of their daily life. Shaker cabinetmakers, master craftsmen trained and working within their own communities, created furniture in rectilinear shapes fashioned from strong woods—maple, cherry, and birch. Subtle color variations of the woods, rubbed to a clean, smooth finish, disguised the physical strength of seemingly brittle shapes. Immaculate spaces were furnished with ingenious and pragmatic forms: beds moved on rollers, chairs were light, and could be hung beside hangers and brushes on the pegboards which lined most rooms. Everything exhibited a plain grace, complementing the contemplative attitudes of the community in its quest for harmony and perfection.

Edward Hicks (AMERICAN, 1780–1849)
Noah's Ark, ABOUT 1846

OIL ON CANVAS, 26½ × 30½"
BEQUEST OF LISA NORRIS ELKINS. 50-92-7

Edward Hicks's painting *Noah's Ark* is based upon a popular lithograph issued by Nathaniel Currier in 1844. But Hicks has added elements of his own invention to clarify the scene and interpret the Biblical story in the light of his profound Quaker faith. Against the threatening sky and somber landscape that dramatize the approaching cataclysm, wild and domestic beasts together move toward the ark with unusual calm, fulfilling a divine purpose. Hicks, who lived in Bucks County, Pennsylvania, and served in the Friends' ministry from 1811 until the end of his life, painted signs and did other kinds of ornamental work to earn his living. Although he disparaged his talent, saying that painting was "one of those trifling, insignificant arts which has never been of substantial advantage to mankind," he painted with humble diligence, depicting historical and religious subjects including his famous "Peaceable Kingdoms," of which more than eighty versions are known to have existed.

Jean-Baptiste-Camille Corot (FRENCH, 1796–1875)

House and Factory of M. Henry, 1833

OIL ON CANVAS, 32⅛ × 39½"
PURCHASED: THE W. P. WILSTACH COLLECTION. W 50-1-1

With the frequent emphasis on Corot as the master of light and atmospheric effects who opened the way for the Impressionists, it is often forgotten that he was born in the eighteenth century and executed the masterpieces of his early maturity in a neoclassical style. Corot was thirty-seven when he was commissioned by a cloth manufacturer in Soissons—a Monsieur Henry—to paint this view of his house and factory. (A second painting was also commissioned to reproduce the countryside as seen from the windows of the factory.) The artist rendered the buildings in steep perspective, with small-scale isolated figures emphatically marking off the vast and monumental space, enclosed from behind by the buildings that cast their shadows across the foreground. The spareness of the image is such, and is so unrelieved, that when a specific detail does occur, for instance, the bell and its shadow on the facade of the factory, it seems of almost startling intensity. During a long and prolific career, Corot's style was to modulate and soften, but he would never lose his devotion to the physicality and immediacy of forms seen in light which already served him so well here.

Joseph Mallord William Turner (ENGLISH, 1775–1851)

Burning of the Houses of Parliament, 1835

OIL ON CANVAS, 36¼ × 48½"
JOHN H. McFADDEN COLLECTION. M 28-1-41

On the evening of October 16, 1834, the British Houses of Parliament caught fire and burned nearly to the ground. A huge crowd gathered to watch on the opposite bank, on Westminster Bridge, and even, for those lucky enough to find a boat, on the Thames itself. Turner stationed himself with the watchful mob and, working rapidly during the night, executed nine watercolors of the fire. From these sketches, essentially color records of the effect of the roaring holocaust against the river and night sky, he made two oil paintings which he exhibited the following year. One of these, now in Cleveland, shows the scene from down the Thames; that shown here portrays the event from almost directly across the river. The fire seems to have compelled Turner to go beyond a literal recording of this extraordinary event to a plane of almost visionary supernaturalism: the crowd sweeps and surges, the bridge is exaggerated (almost metamorphosed) into a lunging form, and violent lights burst forth in the deep autumnal night.

Edouard Manet (FRENCH, 1832–1883)

Le Bon Bock ("Good Beer"), 1873

OIL ON CANVAS, 37 ¼ × 32 ¾"
MR. AND MRS. CARROLL S. TYSON COLLECTION. 63-116-9

When Manet exhibited *Le Bon Bock* at the Salon of 1873, it met with considerable public success, an extremely surprising response given the harsh reception of his earlier works. He had been labeled a dissident, a rebel whose "crude" handling of paint was an intentional affront to the great tradition of French painting; but, finally, with this picture the tide shifted—although only temporarily. The reasons for its success are immediately apparent. The portly, ruddy-cheeked fellow puffing contentedly on his pipe and securely holding his glass of "good Haarlem brew" continues to please in the same way as when the painting was first exhibited. The model was Manet's friend Bellot, an engraver and lithographer who was a frequent visitor (often found in this pose, one imagines) to the Parisian artists' cafe, the Guerbois. Bellot posed more than sixty times for this picture—a fact one would hardly expect from the completed work, which has all the assurance of a swiftly executed canvas.

Thomas Eakins (AMERICAN, 1844–1916)
The Fairman Rogers Four-in-Hand, 1879

OIL ON CANVAS, 24 × 36"
GIVEN BY WILLIAM ALEXANDER DICK. 30-105-1

Fairman Rogers was a keen sportsman, one of the first Philadelphians to own and drive a four-in-hand coach. Rogers is shown, whip in hand, driving with his family in Philadelphia's Fairmount Park. Such a depiction of high style was unusual for Eakins, but he turned to it with his usual interest in the substance of things and the accurate reproduction of figures in motion. The artist made numerous oil sketches and wax models of the horses in preparation for the finished picture. As a result, the character of the scene does not depend upon a veneer of glamour conveyed in a dashing impression; the sleek beauty of the horses, the polished intricacies of harness, the shining coach, and the well-dressed men and women combine into the kind of solid impressiveness that repays a close, appreciative scrutiny of objects of the highest quality. The ultimate effect of such a superb equipage depends upon its harmony in motion, and Eakins shows this aspect as carefully as he does the reflection in a lacquered door or the fringe of a shawl. As the coach spanks through the park, it appears in sharp detail against the muted, softly defined background as if isolated by the admiring gaze of some passerby.

Eduard Charlemont (AUSTRIAN, 1848–1906)

Moorish Chief, ABOUT 1880

OIL ON PANEL, 59⅛ × 38½"
JOHN G. JOHNSON COLLECTION. 951

European taste for elements of North African and Near Eastern culture was firmly established early in the nineteenth century, and with the triumphs of the Romantics in the 1830s and 1840s, pashas and caliphs rivaled traditional gods and goddesses on the Salon walls. Exoticism, mystery, and passion all seem to have been implicit in these subjects; and given their popularity, the taste soon ran shallow. Thus it is surprising that Charlemont, working about 1880, could produce a picture at once so splendidly exotic and so jarring an individual portrait. His means are subtle and knowingly theatrical: the raking light across the figure guarding the passageway, bronze and gold smoldering in the half-lights, the glint of the drawn sword. Charlemont was Viennese, and the intense richness of this work suggests his origins in a city that sustained the best qualities of Romantic opulence until late in the century.

Luigi Frullini (ITALIAN, 1839–1897)
Chair and Footstool, 1875–1876

CARVED WALNUT, AND PAINTED STAMPED AND GILDED LEATHER, HEIGHT 46″
GIVEN BY THE PRESERVATION SOCIETY OF NEWPORT COUNTY, INC. 69-198-2

In 1869, the year of his marriage, George Peabody Wetmore, later a three-term senator from Rhode Island, commissioned the architect Richard Morris Hunt to enlarge the family estate "Château-sur-Mer" at Newport. A young and already internationally recognized Florentine designer, Luigi Frullini, was engaged to decorate the remodeled dining room and library. Frullini conceived and executed the two interiors and their furniture during 1875 and 1876. This chair and footstool formed part of Frullini's dining-room set; like the walls of the room itself, they are upholstered in stamped and gilded Spanish leather. The neo-Renaissance style of the chair, with its animal forms and classical wave and rosette moldings, takes artistic sanction from sixteenth-century prototypes. Yet, in his superb craftsmanship and completely original use of Renaissance vocabulary, Frullini created furniture that ranks among the best produced anywhere during the nineteenth century.

Mary Cassatt (AMERICAN, 1845–1926)
Woman and Child Driving, 1879

OIL ON CANVAS, 35¼ × 51½"
PURCHASED: THE W. P. WILSTACH COLLECTION. W 21-1-1

It is typical of Mary Cassatt's independence of mind that, when she went to Paris in 1866 to continue her studies after four years at the Pennsylvania Academy of the Fine Arts, she found stimulus for her work in the new and controversial art of the day. She admired the paintings of Courbet and Manet and, slightly later, became acquainted with the work of artists who were derisively named "Impressionists" after their first exhibition in 1874. In 1877 Edgar Degas asked her to show her work with the Impressionists, and she became the only American to participate in their exhibitions. *Woman and Child Driving,* painted in 1879 when Mary Cassatt first exhibited with the Impressionists, depicts the artist's sister Lydia with a young niece of Degas, driving in the Bois de Boulogne near Paris. The subject from everyday life and the glowing, loosely brushed color indicate her affinity with the work of the Impressionists. More particularly, the extremely asymmetrical composition of figures balanced by strong patterns of color suggests the influence of Degas, who advised her in her work and with whom she shared a long, occasionally testy friendship.

Edgar-Hilaire-Germain Degas (FRENCH, 1834–1917)

The Ballet Class, ABOUT 1878–1880

OIL ON CANVAS, 32⅛ × 30⅛"
PURCHASED: THE W. P. WILSTACH COLLECTION. W 37-2-1

The world of ballet appealed tremendously to Degas, but curiously, Parisian ballet was at a low ebb just at the time Degas documented it so thoroughly, and the humorously awkward dancers in a *pas de trois* here could well be taken to illustrate its rather flaccid state of affairs. Degas has divided the pictorial space diagonally by a line in the parquet, a line so subtle yet so crucial that the crossing of it by an extended foot seems a clumsy affront. The complex composition has the same tentative balance as the dancer so perilously *en pointe.* Degas is popularly misunderstood as the proponent of grace and balletic poise; nothing could be further from the truth. To capture transient movement and characteristic attributes was his prime concern, and his genius consists in presenting fleeting movement within a work of art which is, in itself, permanent and stable.

Claude Monet (FRENCH, 1840–1926)

Poplars, 1891

OIL ON CANVAS, 36¼ × 29"
GIVEN BY CHESTER DALE. 51-109-1

In 1891 Monet began a series of paintings of the poplars along the river Epte, near the French village of Giverny, where he had purchased a house the year before. His goal was to pursue nature in all its variety, and from the large number of works of this subject, in a broad diversity of colors and compositions, we know that he probed nature with astonishing vigor and system. A neighbor has left us an account of the flat-bottomed boat from which he painted, specially fitted with slots to hold several canvases so that he could quickly shift from one to another as light and weather conditions changed. At one point he was even forced to buy the trees, which the village was auctioning off for timber—thus ensuring that his subjects would continue to stand until the completion of his work. This series of canvases documents Monet's steady, undeviating, and often tormented pursuance of the Impressionist attitude toward recording optical truth, which he and a small group of fellow painters first began practicing in the late 1860s.

Vincent van Gogh (DUTCH, 1853–1890)

Sunflowers, 1888

OIL ON CANVAS, 36⅜ × 28⅝"
MR. AND MRS. CARROLL S. TYSON COLLECTION. 63-116-19

In February of 1888 Vincent van Gogh left Paris and moved to Arles in the south of France. During that summer and the following winter, there occurred the incidents which most nourished his legend—the fight with Gauguin, Van Gogh's mutilation of his own ear, and his recurring lapses into madness. But this was also the culminating period of his career, when he produced some of his most compelling works. Intoxicated by the intense light and colors of Provence, he was finally able to achieve a complete break with the analytic vision of Impressionism and to realize fully his own extraordinarily private, subjective style. This is nowhere more evident than in the "Sunflowers" canvases (there are six in all) on which he worked in August of that year. With acid colors and swift brushstrokes, he animated the coarse abundance and spiky tangle of the flowers with an organic vitality and splendor. In a letter to his brother Theo he wrote of his response to the challenge: "Now to get up heat enough to melt that gold, those flower tones."

Winslow Homer (AMERICAN, 1836–1910)
Huntsman and Dogs, 1891

OIL ON CANVAS, 28¼ × 48″
THE WILLIAM L. ELKINS COLLECTION. E 24-3-8

Winslow Homer's fishing trips to the Adirondacks in 1889 and the early 1890s resulted in a series of brilliant watercolors of the landscape, the wildlife, and the woodsmen of the area. *Huntsman and Dogs* is based upon one of these watercolor studies, and the austere strength of the scene typifies Homer's unsentimental appreciation of life in the wilderness. In the somber atmosphere of a late autumn day, the stolid, angular figure of the young huntsman, his recent success evident in the deer hide and antlers he carries, stands in isolation against the long slope of a burned-over mountain. The energetic movement of the barking dogs contrasts with the immobility of the hunter's figure and emphasizes the silence and barrenness of the landscape.

Thomas Eakins (AMERICAN, 1844–1916)
Portrait of Mrs. William D. Frishmuth, 1900

OIL ON CANVAS, 97 × 72½″
GIVEN BY MRS. THOMAS EAKINS AND MISS MARY A. WILLIAMS. 29·184·7

At a time when fashionable portraitists were expected to flatter their subjects and produce an effect of character that conformed to the current style, Thomas Eakins usually chose his sitters from among his friends and those who interested him and painted them without commission, creating compelling portraits of individual character and physical presence. In this painting of Mrs. William D. Frishmuth, a great collector of colonial and ethnological artifacts, the bright light which emphasizes the strong, tangible forms of Mrs. Frishmuth's face and hands and the severity of her black dress draws attention to her strong gesture and thoughtful expression. An arrangement of her collection of musical instruments creates an exotic setting for the figure of Mrs. Frishmuth, isolating it in the large space of the canvas. The variety of shape and color in the instruments contrasts with the compact volumes and concentrated intelligence of the figure, reinforcing the effect of a self-contained, forceful personality.

Pierre-Auguste Renoir (FRENCH, 1841–1919)

The Bathers, 1887

OIL ON CANVAS, 46⅜ × 67¼"
MR. AND MRS. CARROLL S. TYSON COLLECTION. 63-116-13

In 1886 Renoir, depressed and discouraged with himself and his painting, traveled to Italy. There, after seeing Raphael's paintings and the Roman frescoes at Pompeii, he began to move away from the light-dissolved forms of his Impressionist style, resolving that to continue as an artist he must return to a simpler, more precise and more firmly drawn technique. Renoir called this his "dry manner," which reached its fullest resolution in this painting, begun shortly after his return. It is a picture that posed formidable problems from its very inception, since Renoir so clearly set out to do a masterpiece within the great tradition of the nude. In its scale and formal complexity it is the most ambitious undertaking of his career. The summer light softening the trees and glistening on the water recalls his earlier work, but the figures, undappled by light, have the abundance and grace of goddesses free from time and change.

Augustus Saint-Gaudens (AMERICAN, BORN IRELAND, 1848–1907)
Diana, 1892

COPPER SHEETS, HEIGHT 14′6″
GIVEN BY THE NEW YORK LIFE INSURANCE COMPANY. 32-30-1

Saint-Gaudens created *Diana* as a weathervane for the tower of the first Madison Square Garden in New York. Constructed of thin copper sheets for lightness, originally gilded and with a billowing drapery to catch the wind, this figure of the Roman goddess of the hunt stood as a symbol of the festive spirit of a building designed as a pleasure garden as well as a sports arena. The mythological subject was intended to serve as a link with the great art of the past, but *Diana*'s lithe, athletic grace and slender, elongated proportions were the fashion of the day, and her nudity caused some public furor until the figure acquired the respectability of a landmark. Two versions of the *Diana* were made. When the first, over eighteen feet tall, was found to be out of proportion with the building, this second, smaller version was made and remained in place until the Garden was demolished in 1925.

Paul Cézanne (FRENCH, 1839–1906)

The Large Bathers, 1898–1905

OIL ON CANVAS, 82 × 99″
PURCHASED: THE W. P. WILSTACH COLLECTION. W 37-1-1

During most of his long career, Cézanne disregarded the one subject which, even throughout the nineteenth century, was considered one of the highest concerns of art—the nude. Landscapes, still lifes, and portraits were by far his greatest concern; occasionally, however, he painted small studies of nudes in landscapes. Toward the end of his life, he resolved to undertake the subject of the nude on a large scale and executed three very different versions of *The Large Bathers*. (The two others are now in the National Gallery in London and the Barnes Foundation in Merion, Pennsylvania.) The massiveness of the figures and their placement within a proscenium arch of trees speak as much to the traditions of sculpture as of painting. The sober beauty of the color (blue, green, and ocher) and the assured sparseness of its application create a work of astonishing economy and monumentality. It stands as the final—and perhaps most moving—testament of Cézanne's search for the basic geometry of nature, and as the first masterpiece of classical painting in the twentieth century.

Alfred Stieglitz (AMERICAN, 1864–1946)
Early New York: The City of Ambition, 1910

PHOTOGRAPH, 4⅛ × 3¼"
THE ALFRED STIEGLITZ COLLECTION. 49-18-47

This is one of Alfred Stieglitz's many photographs of New York cityscapes, in which he conveys the vitality and the tempo of the city, as suggested by the clouds of smoke billowing from tall, erect buildings outlined against the sky and from the ferryboat on the river below. Stieglitz offers proof of the effectiveness of the photographic medium in making a clear, straightforward visual statement, devoid of embellishment and stripped of all disguises. There are no additions or subtractions, no alterations or distortions, but only what was seen through the lens of the camera. His rare sensitivity in selecting a composition that is factual yet satisfying emphasizes the aesthetic possibilities of the medium, giving validity to his lifetime crusade to promote photography as an independent art in America.

Henri Rousseau (FRENCH, 1844–1910)

Carnival Evening, 1886

OIL ON CANVAS, 46 × 35¼"
THE LOUIS E. STERN COLLECTION. 63·181·64

A couple dressed as Pierrot and Columbine, pantomime characters from the Italian *commedia dell'arte*, stand on a rise before a wintry forest. Three delicate clouds hover above a solid bank of mist. A single streetlight glows incongruously in the cool poetry of moonlight and an unexplained face leers out from a pergola. The scene is totally mysterious, a vision drawn from the imagination. Rousseau turned his facility for observation and his sophisticated sense of design not to the outside world but rather to a private, very gentle, inner reality. The charm and unique quality of his work would only be discovered and praised some fifteen years later by avant-garde critics and artists, among them Picasso; but when this painting was exhibited at the Salon des Indépendants in 1886, no one seems to have taken notice of it. With no formal training, Rousseau bravely (and determinedly) entered the exhibition solely on the strength of his own conviction of the worth of his paintings and their essential honesty.

Henry van de Velde (BELGIAN, 1863–1957)

Meissen Tea Set, GERMAN, 1904

HARD-PASTE PORCELAIN, TEAPOT HEIGHT 6⅛″
GIVEN BY THE FRIENDS OF THE MUSEUM. 73-94-5

Inspired by the efforts of the English Arts and Crafts movement to restore high standards of craftsmanship and artistry to the decorative arts, Henry van de Velde abandoned his painting career in 1893 to become an industrial arts designer. From 1899 to 1914, he worked exclusively in Germany, where he designed architecture, furniture, graphics, textiles, and metalwork at the School of Applied Arts in Weimar, which he founded in 1902. It was also in 1902 that ceramics designed by Van de Velde were first exhibited, and their success encouraged the patronage of Germany's most important porcelain factory, the Royal Saxon China Manufactory at Meissen. Within the next five years, Van de Velde designed two porcelain table services for Meissen— this tea set having been part of the first service. The elegance of the streamlined forms, heightened by the curving lines of the dark-blue and grey decoration, confirms Van de Velde's place at the forefront of the Art Nouveau movement, which introduced the first original ornamental vocabulary since the Rococo style of the eighteenth century.

Constantin Brancusi (RUMANIAN, 1876–1957)
The Kiss, 1912

LIMESTONE, HEIGHT 23″
THE LOUISE AND WALTER ARENSBERG COLLECTION. 50-134-4

Although he lived in Paris for over fifty years, Brancusi retained the craftsman's skill and love for materials and the sense of simple, almost primitive form which were deeply rooted in his Rumanian peasant origins. *The Kiss* was one of his favorite themes, of which at least six variations are known: an earlier, more naturalistic version serves as a gravestone in a Paris cemetery, and the same motif appeared as late as 1938, abstracted and enlarged, in an architectural project for a park in Rumania. The Philadelphia sculpture is severely formal, yet tender, in its presentation of two figures clasped together, their unity expressed by the single block of stone into which their simple contours are incised. Not passion but permanence is expressed in the barely differentiated, gently interlocking forms of the lovers, so far removed from Rodin's sensuous and romantic treatment of the same theme. Brancusi's *Kiss* has a quiet monumentality which renders it archaic in feeling, yet made it a work of startling modernity for 1912.

Pablo Picasso (SPANISH, 1881–1973)

Self-Portrait, 1906

OIL ON CANVAS, 36¼ × 28¾"
A. E. GALLATIN COLLECTION. 50-1-1

Despite his fascination with portraiture, which led him to explore the features of friends, mistresses, and children in numerous paintings and sketches, Picasso rarely turned his penetrating gaze directly on himself, as in this vision of the young painter on the eve of the Cubist revolution. We are not admitted into the artist's private emotions but, rather, confronted by a boldly simplified figure whose forceful head resembles the blunted, staring faces of pre-Roman Iberian stone sculpture, which Picasso admired at the time. There is little in this calm portrait to suggest the formal complexities and violent structural distortions soon to emerge in Picasso's early Cubist pictures; yet it is equally far from the literary melancholy which pervaded the sinuous forms of his Blue Period. Here Picasso chose to present himself not in the act of painting, but in the still more essential act of contemplating the world he is about to transmute into art.

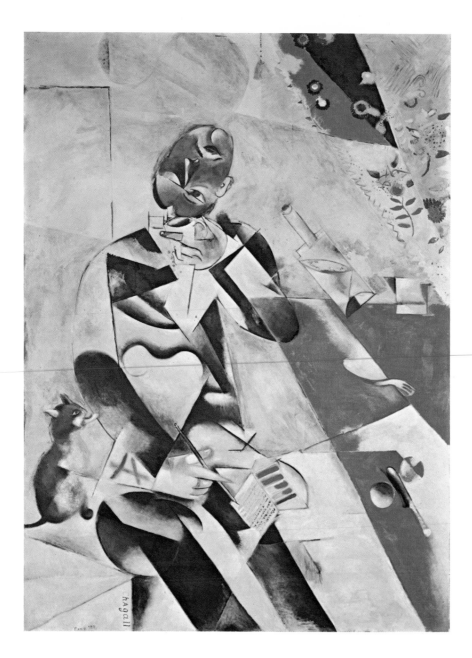

Marc Chagall (FRENCH, BORN RUSSIA, 1889)
Half-Past Three (The Poet), 1912

OIL ON CANVAS, 77½ × 57½"
THE LOUISE AND WALTER ARENSBERG COLLECTION. 50-134-36

The portrait of the poet Mazin, Chagall's neighbor in the Parisian artist's settlement where he lived from 1912 to 1914, evolved into one of the most lighthearted and lyrical paintings of the Cubist period. Chagall joins Cubist faceting of solid form and spatial ambiguity with his own narrative fantasy and brilliant sense of color. Derived from an earlier, more conventional portrayal of Mazin seated by a table drinking coffee, *Half-Past Three* plays fast and loose with the laws of gravity and perspective. A bottle hovers precariously at the poet's elbow, a little green cat (perhaps a feline muse?) licks his arm, and the flowers in the curtain overhead appear about to spill over into space. The source of all this madness is surely in the poet's head, which, bright green and topsy-turvy, floats above his blue shoulders as he writes in the delirium of poetic inspiration.

Juan Gris (SPANISH, 1887–1927)

Still Life before an Open Window (La Place Ravignan), 1915

OIL ON CANVAS, 45 ⅞ × 35 ⅛"
THE LOUISE AND WALTER ARENSBERG COLLECTION. 50-134-95

At the outset of their complex analysis of three-dimensional forms in space about 1910, the Cubists, particularly Picasso and Braque, restricted their subjects to still-life arrangements or single figures in a shallow space. By 1915 they were expanding their visual explorations to include larger vistas, and in that year Gris achieved one of the most lyrical interminglings of exterior and interior space in this painting of his studio with an open window. The objects assembled on the tilted tabletop—a bottle of Médoc, fruit dish, carafe, wine glass, newspaper, and book—appear transfigured by shafts of colored light; the unearthly blue that bathes the square outside the window passes into the room and tints the scroll-patterned wallpaper. The leaves of the trees beyond the window spread a magical shade across the whole composition, and the viewer feels himself in the presence of a poetic enchantment rare in Gris's precise, analytical art.

Wassily Kandinsky (RUSSIAN, 1866–1944)
Improvisation No. 29, 1912

OIL ON CANVAS, 41⅝ × 38″
THE LOUISE AND WALTER ARENSBERG COLLECTION. 50-134-102

In his series of paintings entitled "Improvisations," Kandinsky pursued a gradual course toward abstraction, eliminating recognizable references to the natural world and evolving a vocabulary of colors and forms with which to express spiritual feelings. In this painting, also called *The Swan*, vestiges of landscape linger in its swirling shapes: perhaps a purple wave in the lower left, the long curved neck of the swan in the center. Kandinsky did not rigidly control his tendency to introduce natural forms in the "Improvisations," since he sought for a "largely unconscious, spontaneous expression of inner character." Yet this buoyant, joyous composition is by no means haphazard, for the painter balances forms and orchestrates colors until every area of his canvas comes alive. When, in 1913, the English critic Roger Fry saw this painting with two others by Kandinsky, they struck him as "pure visual music."

Charles Demuth (AMERICAN, 1883–1935)

The Green Dancer, 1916

WATERCOLOR AND PENCIL ON PAPER, 11 × 8″
THE SAMUEL S. WHITE, 3RD, AND VERA WHITE COLLECTION. 67-30-21

A man of consummate elegance who delighted in bohemian company, Demuth was able to capture the haunting quality of his world and its nightlife in his many theatrical scenes, especially those of vaudeville performers and circus acrobats. In *The Green Dancer*, one of the finest of these scenes, the ingenious device of two harsh intersecting spotlights that catch the dancers in the midst of their act results in one of Demuth's most striking compositions. Nevertheless, this watercolor is not without a touch of ambivalence, perhaps even of irony, since its frenetic mood and the slightly inane expressions frozen on the dancers' faces expose the tinsel superficiality of the music-hall stage.

Marcel Duchamp (AMERICAN, BORN FRANCE, 1887–1968)

The Bride Stripped Bare by Her Bachelors, Even (The "Large Glass"), 1915–1923

OIL, VARNISH, LEAD FOIL, LEAD WIRE, AND DUST ON TWO GLASS PANELS
(CRACKED), 9′1¼″ × 5′9¼″
BEQUEST OF KATHERINE S. DREIER. 52-98-1

In 1912 Duchamp began to jot down notes hinting at a project that was to preoccupy him for the next decade. Years were spent in preparing sketches and plans, and inventing idiosyncratic methods of measurement and composition depending on chance operations. Between 1915 and 1923, Duchamp carefully transferred his plans to two large glass panels, and in 1936 he reassembled the fragments when the work accidentally broke. The complex erotic saga of the Bride (in the upper panel) and the Bachelors (who inhabit the lower one) is not apparent in the *Glass* itself but only in Duchamp's published notes for this enigmatic work. Obeying its creator's dictum that the "*Spectators* . . . make the picture," the *Large Glass* reflects the viewer's own image, and superimposes a static diagram of love "machinery" upon the shifting world around it.

Marcel Duchamp (AMERICAN, BORN FRANCE, 1887–1968)

Nude Descending a Staircase, No. 2, 1912

OIL ON CANVAS, 58 × 35″
THE LOUISE AND WALTER ARENSBERG COLLECTION. 50·134·59

It may seem surprising today that this elegantly streamlined abstraction of a figure descending a
flight of steps would have provoked a scandalized uproar in Paris and New York just before
World War I. When Duchamp submitted his painting to the Salon des Indépendants in Paris in
1912, even his avant-garde Cubist colleagues found it disturbing and forced him to withdraw it.
When a year later he sent it to the first great international exhibition of modern art in America,
New York's celebrated "Armory Show," it became a *cause célèbre*, the butt of endless jokes, earn-
ing such sobriquets as "explosion in a shingle factory" and "subway at rush hour." Inspired by
photographic studies of motion, Duchamp sought to represent a moving human figure through
a series of similar forms distributed in jerky sequence across the canvas. To clinch the matter, he
inscribed the title in bold letters on the painting itself—an unconventional and possibly ironic
addition which may have contributed to his Cubist friends' unease.

97

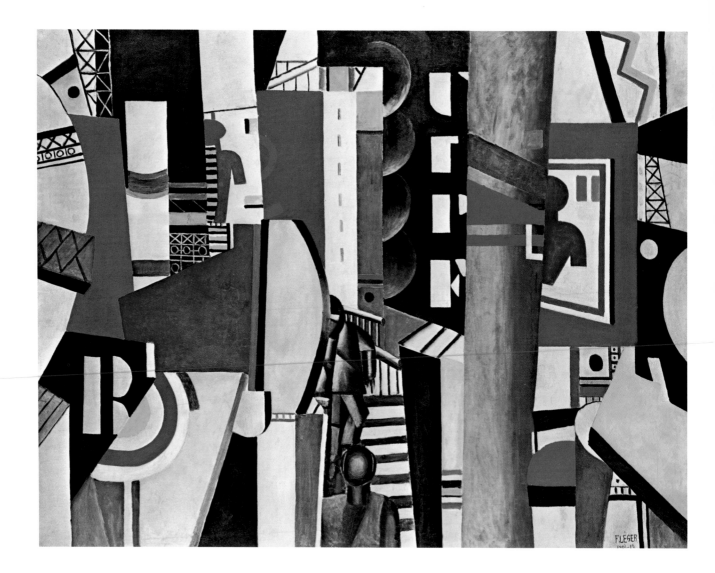

Fernand Léger (FRENCH, 1881–1955)
The City, 1919

OIL ON CANVAS, 7′7″ × 9′9½″
A. E. GALLATIN COLLECTION. 52-61-58

Léger, a fervent apostle of modernism, found the rapid pace and commercial dynamism of the Machine Age a stimulus to his art. Uninterested in capturing the variable effects of weather and light associated with Impressionism, he hailed the advertising billboard "shouting in a timid landscape" as the impetus for a bold new direction in painting. The modern city was an ideal theme for Léger, and this masterpiece of late Cubism was the culmination of numerous studies and several years of work. The sights and sounds, the rhythms and excitement of urban life are compressed into a panorama of painted shapes and signs. Here and there amid flat planes of bright color, we glimpse puffs of smoke, a fragment of a poster, the scaffolding for a new building, and the ironwork of a bridge. In the lower center, two grey robot-like figures, denizens of this dynamic new world, go about their business. The tightly organized composition is made up of fragments like "frames" of a film—a new medium which Léger much admired—and abstracted details of the city are reconstituted into a boldly simplified yet endlessly animated cinematic whole.

Pablo Picasso (SPANISH, 1881–1973)

Three Musicians, 1921

OIL ON CANVAS, 80 × 74″
A. E. GALLATIN COLLECTION. 52-61-96

During the summer of 1921, Picasso painted the two versions of this picture which constitute the culminating statement of Synthetic Cubism. One of the pair, now in The Museum of Modern Art in New York, also shows the musicians seated at a table, but the shadowy form of a large dog lurks beneath it. Though less mysterious, the Philadelphia painting is more complex than its companion piece, comprising a veritable encyclopedia of Cubist devices and visual tricks. The three *commedia dell'arte* characters, masked and sporting rather sinister smiles, are arranged in the shallow picture space like actors on a narrow stage. From left to right: Harlequin holds a violin and bow, Pierrot plays a recorder with sheet music unfolded before him, and a monk in cowl and corded robe holds an accordion. The imposing scale and intricate balance of the composition, combined with the venerable tradition of the subject, make this Picasso's formidable challenge to the great Salon paintings of the past. But the brilliant interplay of color and pattern and its witty distortion of form assure us that the music from this Cubist concert is as modern as jazz.

Georges Braque (FRENCH, 1882–1963)
Musical Forms (Guitar and Clarinet), 1918

PASTED PAPER, CORRUGATED CARDBOARD, CHARCOAL, AND GOUACHE ON CARDBOARD, 30⅜ × 37⅜″
THE LOUISE AND WALTER ARENSBERG COLLECTION. 50-134-28

With the simplest still-life elements and the most ordinary materials, Braque achieves a triumph in this collage, which is at once monumental and supremely elegant. The interplay between recognizable forms and abstract shapes and colors is characteristic of Braque's delight in creating a purely pictorial world: "Objects are created for a new purpose . . . that of playing a part in a picture." The corrugated-cardboard clarinet and wood-grain paper guitar are subjected to paradoxical treatment: at once thrust into relief by the bold black shapes that can be read as their shadows, yet flattened by the little sheet of music paper which overlaps the guitar but willfully vanishes behind the clarinet. Braque has used his charcoal pencil with brilliant economy; two ellipses form the sound hole of the guitar and the mouth of the clarinet, and eight parallel strokes suggest music paper. Rarely have collage elements been allowed such freedom from the drawn line. The visual rhythms Braque creates by "rhyming" forms and contours with one another are the pictorial equivalent of the musical harmony evoked by the silent instruments.

Paul Klee (SWISS, 1879–1940)
Fish Magic, 1925

OIL ON CLOTH MOUNTED ON BOARD, 30⅜ × 38½"
THE LOUISE AND WALTER ARENSBERG COLLECTION. 50-134-112

Paul Klee believed that a continuing creative dialogue with nature was essential to the formation of an artist; in the artist's "thinking eye," outward sight and inward vision should mingle, and his paintings should parallel the natural world of which he himself is part. *Fish Magic* gathers many of Klee's fondest images into a nocturnal dream: plants, mysterious suns or stars, whimsical little figures of a girl and a clown. The painting is at once a flat dark canvas, richly textured and inscribed with mysterious signs, and a deep pool of darkness in which luminous forms float and where time itself is suspended. Do the fish swim in air, or do the flowers bloom underwater? Such prosaic questions falter before the enchanted spell which balances all elements in a tranquil equilibrium. The fish themselves, which appear in several of his paintings of this period, caught Klee's imagination with their elemental mode of being, effortlessly at one with their environment. Perhaps he also found, in their simplified forms, a simile for the shape of the open eye, and therefore an image of vision itself.

101

Joan Miró (SPANISH, BORN 1893)
Dog Barking at the Moon, 1926

OIL ON CANVAS, 28⅞ × 36½"
A. E. GALLATIN COLLECTION. 52-61-82

When *Dog Barking at the Moon*—one of the first works by Miró to be on public view in this country—was shown in New York in 1929, it was greeted with a humorous uproar in the press. Perhaps the picture's odd simplicity caught viewers off guard. Composed of only a few elements carefully placed against two flat areas of color, the night landscape takes on a vast scale within a comparatively small canvas, as a limitless black sky touches the undulating brown earth. The dog, the flying wisp of moon which tantalizes him, and the slender ladder which stretches to the stars might be figments of a dream—and in 1929 the public was not accustomed to seeing dreams painted with such poetic license. Although the picture records an event, nothing within it moves, and the dog barks in a soundless realm of the imagination.

Salvador Dali (SPANISH, BORN 1904)

Soft Construction with Boiled Beans (Premonition of Civil War), 1936

OIL ON CANVAS, 39⅜ × 39″
THE LOUISE AND WALTER ARENSBERG COLLECTION. 50-134-41

In this monstrous vision of a humanoid monument, hideously malformed and preying upon itself, Dali applied his brilliant technical skill as a painter and his Surrealist method of depicting fantastic dreamworld subjects with a heightened realism to the imminent tragedy of the Spanish Civil War. Against a dramatic, clouded sky, the Soft Construction rises as a grisly memorial of man's inhumanity to man, its immensity emphasized by the diminutive professorial figure of a bearded gentleman who inspects the distorted hand at the lower left of the picture. Rarely do Dali's hallucinatory images provoke such profoundly grim and painful sensations as this particular "materialization of concrete irrationality."

Pablo Picasso (SPANISH, 1881–1973)
Man with a Lamb, 1943–1944

BRONZE, HEIGHT 79½"
GIVEN BY R. STURGIS AND
MARION B. F. INGERSOLL. 68-115-8

One of Picasso's most important sculptures began as the figure of a shepherd in a series of drawings he executed in 1942. As he developed the idea, Picasso felt that the powerful image demanded to be realized in sculpture, and on a large scale. A metal armature was constructed in his Paris studio in 1943; then, after several months of thought, the artist swiftly built up the sculpture from wet clay within the course of just two afternoons, while his friend the poet Paul Eluard watched in amazement and admiration. This is the first of only three bronze casts of the work: Picasso reserved the second for himself and gave the third to the little town of Vallauris on the French Riviera, where he had established a ceramic studio in 1948. The impressive scale of this work and its sober dignity set it apart from the wildly fantastic, witty, or graceful sculptural shapes the artist produced before and since. Conceived during World War II, and now presiding—as one version does—over a small-town marketplace, *Man with a Lamb* may represent an offering to peace as great as *Guernica*'s revelation of the horrors of war.

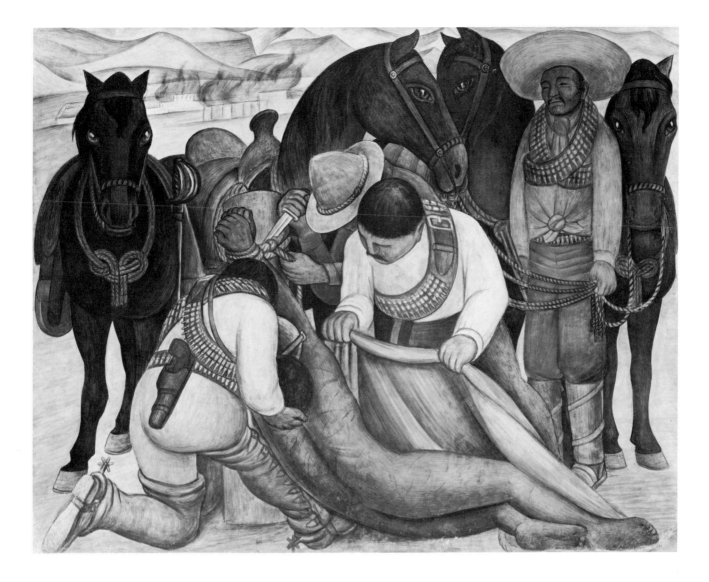

Diego Rivera (MEXICAN, 1886–1957)
Liberation of the Peon, 1931

FRESCO ON PLASTER, 74 × 95"
GIVEN BY MR. AND MRS. HERBERT CAMERON MORRIS. 43-46-1

When he returned to Mexico in 1921 after fourteen years of travel and study in Europe, Rivera devoted his energies to portraying the history and revolutionary struggles of his countrymen. Between 1922 and 1927 he completed his first great fresco cycle on the walls of the Ministry of Education building in Mexico City. The *Liberation of the Peon* is one scene from that series, re-created on portable panels for Rivera's one-man exhibition in 1931 at The Museum of Modern Art in New York. The subject is as grimly stirring as the ballads sung in Mexico at the time: soldiers gently releasing the inert form of a peasant who has been bound to a post and flogged. In the background, the hacienda of a wealthy landowner has been set afire. Rivera's bold, simplified style and earth colors, joined with his explosive subject matter, immediately achieved widespread success. On the strength of paintings like this one and his avowed sympathy for the popular cause, he was urged as a candidate for the presidency of Mexico. Once as he passed a large gathering of peasants and workers in the streets, a voice was heard to call out, "Diego, here at last are your paintings!"

Andrew Wyeth (AMERICAN, BORN 1917)

Ground-Hog Day, 1959

TEMPERA ON MASONITE, 31 × 31¼"
GIVEN BY HENRY F. DUPONT AND MRS. JOHN WINTERSTEEN. 59-102-1

Within a circle of farmland in the gently sloping hills around Chadds Ford, Pennsylvania, Andrew Wyeth found inspiration for an art at once filled with intensely private emotion and yet produced with painstaking, almost relentless attention to detail. Perhaps the center of that green-grey world is the white farmhouse of Wyeth's old friend Karl Kuerner. In *Ground-Hog Day* Wyeth painted the Kuerners' kitchen, a room he had known for years, crowded with the myriad invisible associations of a place where a small group of people gather daily. We see only a cup, a plate, and a knife laid out for lunch on a pristine cloth. Wintry sunshine filtering through a window still closed against the cold provides the sole drama, foreboding six more weeks of winter weather should the ground hog chance to see his shadow on this February day. Yet this empty corner of a kitchen is redolent with human presence, lonely, close to the familiar earth of the slope which rises to shut out any view of the sky. Wyeth encloses the viewer in a timeless moment between the barrenness of winter and the promise of spring.

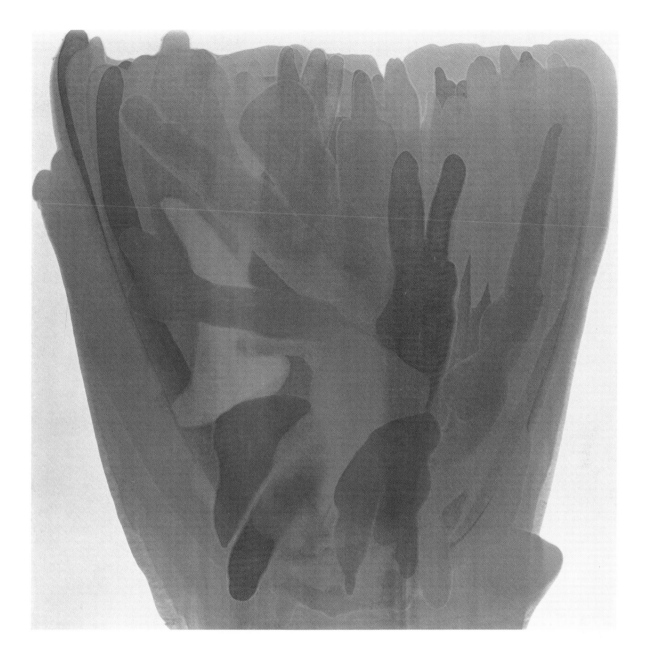

Morris Louis (AMERICAN, 1912–1962)
Beth, 1960

ACRYLIC RESIN PAINT ON CANVAS, 8′9″ × 8′10¼″
PURCHASED: ADELE HAAS TURNER AND BEATRICE PASTORIUS TURNER FUND. 66-172-1

Within eight years, from the time he discovered the technical means to achieve his coloristic aim until his death in 1962, Morris Louis created a remarkably rich and compressed body of work. His technique throughout remained essentially the same: pouring thinned acrylic pigment onto unprimed canvas and tilting it until the color soaked into the desired configuration. *Beth* belongs to a series of transitional works called "Florals," which fall between his "Veil" paintings, with their superimposed layers of color built up into monolithic images, and his last works, in which colors are separated into individual streams on a white field. The forms in this painting are built up of successive waves of color, contained within a large veil-like contour but with distinct outlines like the petals of some giant flower. Color is the single forming element, fusing with the bare canvas so that the eye passes through layer upon layer of a purely optical space—inaccessible to the sense of touch but endlessly absorbing to the mind.

Jacques Lipchitz (AMERICAN, BORN LITHUANIA, 1891–1973)

Prometheus Strangling the Vulture, 1944

BRONZE, HEIGHT 96½″
PURCHASED: LISA NORRIS ELKINS FUND. 52-8-1

The theme of Prometheus, the mythic hero who dared to steal fire from the gods for the benefit of man, runs through Lipchitz's work like a refrain. His first important realization of it came in a major project for the Paris World's Fair in 1936–1937, when he worked from a model (a rare practice for Lipchitz) to create a gigantic, powerfully realistic figure. He returned to the theme in the early 1940s in a large work done for the facade of a building in Rio de Janeiro. Through a tragic error, the finished sculpture was cast in a size far too small for its huge site, but Lipchitz found some consolation in the success of this other smaller version when it was awarded a prize at an exhibition in Philadelphia. Here, Prometheus appears as a forceful, muscular figure in the act of destroying the bird of prey sent to punish his independence. He wears the Phrygian cap, which Lipchitz saw as the symbol of democracy. In the dynamic, billowing forms of man and bird locked in combat, Lipchitz expressed his vision of the perpetual struggle of mankind for "the victory of light over darkness, of education over ignorance."

Alexander Calder (AMERICAN, BORN 1898)

Ghost, 1963

PAINTED SHEET METAL AND METAL RODS, HEIGHT 24'
PURCHASED: NEW MEMBERS FUND. 65-47-1

In the mid-1930s, while certain Surrealists painted dream pictures of biomorphic forms populating vividly colored fields or floating in underwater worlds, Alexander Calder began to set similar shapes adrift in real space. His mobiles move in the same air that we do; any passing breeze sets them on a controlled yet meandering course, capable of infinite variations. In contriving the precise balance of the separate metal shapes, Calder joins his knowledge of mechanics to the whimsical laws of chance. With its long graceful tail that trails downward, *Ghost* is a rarity among Calder's usually horizontal configurations. In the dimness of a vast hall it emerges like an apparition, altering the surrounding space as its white planes first show their curving profiles and then appear to vanish when they turn at right angles to the eye. A flexible skeleton, a sea creature, a slow shower of white petals—Calder's sculpture nudges our familiar world over the boundary into fantasy.

Robert Rauschenberg (AMERICAN, BORN 1925)

Estate, 1963

PHOTO-SILKSCREEN AND OIL ON CANVAS, 96 × 70"
GIVEN BY THE FRIENDS OF THE MUSEUM. 67-88-1

Drawn to what he once called the "gap" between art and life, Rauschenberg often incorporates fragments of the real world into his work. His earlier paintings are filled with objects actually attached to the canvas, but in *Estate* the use of collage has expanded into a new technique. Photographs and sections of newsprint are transferred to silkscreens and then printed on his canvas as ghostly images; a number of these images reappear in several paintings, with their effect varying as they are juxtaposed, repeated, or virtually obliterated with paint. Perhaps a commentary on the confusing panorama of New York or on the explosive forces of our time, *Estate* links a series of dynamic vertical references (a rocket launching, a lamp post, the Statue of Liberty) with an unexpected vista of the Sistine Chapel and the quiet, repeated image of a glass of water. With vigorous brushstrokes Rauschenberg fuses the disparate elements into a vital whole, and the shock waves from the rocket seem to spread until the facade of the city cracks and bursts into a blaze of colored paint.

Tom Wesselmann (AMERICAN, BORN 1931)
Bedroom Painting No. 7, 1967–1969

OIL ON CANVAS, 78 × 87″
PURCHASED: ADELE HAAS TURNER AND BEATRICE PASTORIUS TURNER FUND. 72-156-1

The huge scale of the billboard, the enticing images and succulent colors of advertising display, Madison Avenue's search for the item with the most "popular appeal" all served as inspiration and provocation to American artists in the 1960s. Wesselmann has loaded each element in *Bedroom Painting No. 7* with as much clarity and "message" as it can bear: the reddest nail polish, the softest fake leopardskin, the most seductive toes. Everything is bigger and better than life, like a Technicolor close-up on a giant screen, and yet carefully organized into areas of flat, bright color painted with consummate skill. The isolated, almost abstracted images make a complete painting; although we see only a fraction of the "Great American Nude" whom Wesselmann has painted in so many poses, her toes alone somehow convey the full impact of the overwhelming glamour she embodies.

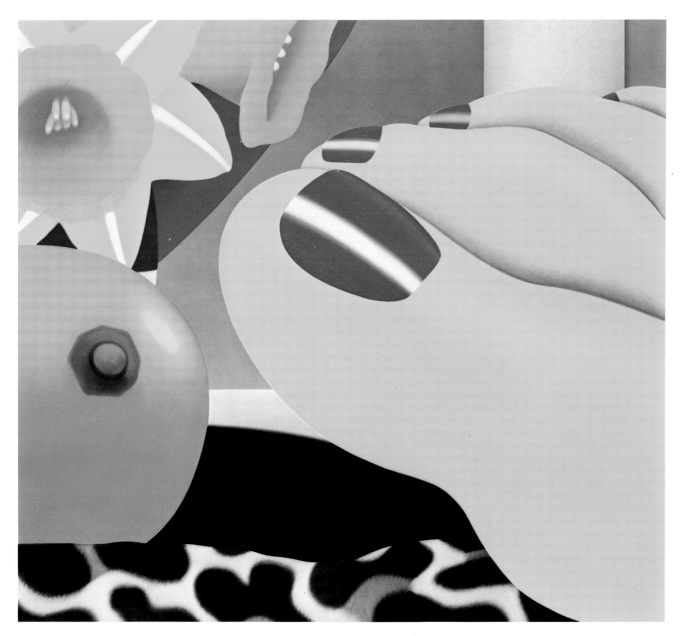

EDITOR'S NOTE

This volume is presented as an introduction to the wealth of material collected during the first century of the Philadelphia Museum of Art. The illustrations are of objects within the Museum itself; neither the three historic houses in Fairmount Park that it maintains (Mount Pleasant, Cedar Grove, and the Letitia Street House), nor the sculpture in the Rodin Museum, which it administers, were considered for presentation here. Selecting 104 works from among the half-million objects in the Museum—by no means a simple task—has offered a pleasant challenge to the staff to reassess their own ideas as to what the "treasures" of the collections are. The objects finally chosen were culled from among those suggested by the curatorial staff as well as from those which throughout the years have continually excited the imagination of great numbers of visitors. It has not been our purpose to ensure that every aspect of the collection has been represented nor that every major donor has been cited.

One of the unique aspects of the Museum is its many architectural interiors fully integrated into a presentation of the artistic achievements of their periods. These rooms have been favored, at times to the exclusion of perhaps more important individual objects of similar styles. Space has permitted only the listing of the source of the architectural elements; our gratitude is extended here to the generous donors of the various furnishings of these rooms.

The commentaries accompanying each illustration were contributed by the following members of the Museum's scholarly community: Anne d'Harnoncourt, Eda Diskant, David DuBon, Charles Grant Ellis, Felice Fischer, Beatrice B. Garvan, Kathryn B. Hiesinger, Stella Kramrisch, Jean Gordon Lee, Elsie S. McGarvey, Kneeland McNulty, Ann Percy, Joseph J. Rishel, Darrel Sewell, and Caroline P. Wistar.

G.H.M.

Photographs by A. J. Wyatt, Staff Photographer, except cover and pages 7, 8, 10, 14, 20, 21, 24, 29, 32, 33, 37, 43, 44, 48, 54, 56, 57, 58, 60, 62–66, 68, 70, 77, 85, 109 by Will Brown; pages 22, 23, 25 by Tom Meehan; page 31 by Otto Nelson; page 96 by Malcolm Varon; pages 50, 104 by Murray Weiss.

EDITOR: GEORGE H. MARCUS
DESIGNER: JOSEPH BOURKE DEL VALLE
COMPOSITION BY A. COLISH INC., MOUNT VERNON, N.Y.
PRINTED BY LEBANON VALLEY OFFSET COMPANY, ANNVILLE, PA.
BOUND BY COMPLETE BOOKS COMPANY, PHILADELPHIA, PA.